KU-265-443

SAVE SAM

ALISTAIR BROWN

CHRISTIAN FOCUS PUBLICATIONS

© 1993 Alistair Brown
ISBN 1 85792 021 X

Published by
Christian Focus Publications Ltd
Geanies House, Fearn, Ross-shire,
IV20 1TW, Scotland, Great Britain.

Cover design by Donna Macleod
Cover illustration by Mike Taylor

Printed and bound in Great Britain by Cox
& Wyman Ltd, Reading, Berks.

All rights reserved. No part of this publication
may be reproduced, stored in a retrieval system,
or transmitted, in any form or by any means,
electronic, mechanical, photocopying, recording
or otherwise, without the prior permission of
Christian Focus Publications.

CONTENTS

Chapter 1

"Please tell me," begged Wendy. "I'd really like to know and I promise I won't tell anyone else."

Helen Shaw smiled at her friend Wendy Jones. It was precisely Wendy's nature to be talkative and inquisitive, so unlike Helen. Hers was a quiet nature, often preferring her own company and keeping her thoughts to herself. But Wendy was special, and Helen shared things with her that she told to no-one else.

School was over for the day, and the two eleven-year-olds were walking slowly homewards. "Why is my English essay mark so important?" Helen teased.

"I saw the look on the teacher's face when he handed back your paper. He was really pleased. I could tell."

Helen grinned. He *had* been pleased.

"All right," she said. "I got eighteen out of twenty for it."

"What! Eighteen out of twenty!" shouted Wendy.

"Ssh! I don't want the whole world to know."

"But that's amazing. I've never heard of anyone getting such a high mark before. What did you write about?"

"Wait until we get out of this playground, and away from everyone else and I'll tell you," Helen replied patiently.

Out the gates they went, other pupils disappearing down various roads. Sometimes people stood around chatting for ages after school, but this was Friday afternoon and everyone wanted to get as far from school as possible and start enjoying their weekend. Gradually the stream of pupils thinned, and Helen was willing to talk about her essay again.

"The title we were given was simply, 'My pet' so I wrote about what it was like to have a dog."

Wendy looked puzzled. "You don't have a dog."

"But I know what it would be like. Well, at least I think I do. I've read library books about dogs, and cut out little articles from my Mum's magazines. When the teacher gave out the essay title I told him I didn't have a pet of my own, and asked if I could just imagine what it would be like."

"So he didn't mind?"

"No. In fact he said it would be a good test of my imagination."

"You've always had plenty of that. And your essay must have been good."

They were coming near to a road junction, and that was where they had to go different ways. Helen lived just outside the town, while Wendy's house wasn't far from the centre. They stopped to talk for a few more minutes.

Helen asked, "Doing anything special this weekend?"

"Yes! I didn't get a chance to tell you earlier, and I only found out myself last night. Dad's boss has paid him a bonus because he's met some sales target or something like that. Anyway, for once he's not going to be working, and we're going away to a hotel."

"That sounds great." Helen felt a touch of jealousy, but she hid it well. "I hope you have a fantastic time."

"We will!" Wendy went on. "The hotel has its own tennis courts, pool table, swimming pool, sauna…the lot! I'm going to enjoy myself." She glanced at her watch.

"Oops, I'd better run. I'm supposed to have my bag packed so we can leave as soon as Dad gets home. Bye!"

"Bye!" Helen called, as her friend disappeared. She turned the other way, along the road leading out of town.

She walked slowly. Her mood had changed. Half an hour before she'd been on top of the world because of the mark her essay had been given. Now she felt quite sad.

'Am I jealous of Wendy?' she asked herself. She didn't mean to be. Really she was pleased for her best friend, because usually Wendy's Dad spent so much time working that she hardly saw him. He went out each morning before she was up, and often came home at night after she was in bed. Sometimes he had to stay away from home for several days on business trips. On top of that, more often than not he was back in his office at weekends. No wonder he'd earned a bonus. At least he was using it to take his family away.

'I wouldn't mind if we could go away sometime, though,' she mused. But she smiled to herself even as she thought it. Her family would never be going off to a posh hotel even for one night. Quite often Mum hardly had the money to pay for the groceries. Sometimes Dad didn't buy a paper if an unexpected bill had come in. Her father worked as hard as anyone. She knew that. It was just that his firm didn't pay very much, and there was never overtime to allow him to earn any more. All the same, she was glad he was home every evening and weekend. That mattered more to her.

'But it would be nice, just someday, to have money for a few luxuries as well,' she said to herself. She turned off the road, and trudged down the long, pot-holed lane towards home. It looked like it was going to be just one more humdrum weekend around the house. Wendy would play her tennis and lie in her sauna. Helen would help Mum, do some schoolwork, perhaps go for a walk. Nothing out of the usual would happen.

Or so she thought...

* * * *

Helen rolled over in bed, and buried her head under a mountain of bedclothes. Bright sunshine streaming through her window told her it was morning. Why had it come so early? Her tired body felt like it was still the middle of the night.

At least there was no need to rush out of bed like she often had to do on other days. This was Saturday, and that meant no school. With Wendy gone for the weekend, there was nothing for her to do.

But sleep wouldn't come again. Helen was well and truly awake, like it or not. She surfaced briefly to glance at her bedside clock. It was 8.00 a.m. Mum would be up by now, but not Dad. Saturday morning was his day to lie in for as long as he could.

Helen dug herself out of her bedcovers, and found the sunshine was warm. That encouraged her, and she convinced herself that maybe it was going to be not such a bad day after all.

An hour later and breakfast was over. "What am I going to do today Mum?" she asked.

Mrs Shaw had her arms in the kitchen sink, clearing the early morning debris of dishes and cups. "I'm sure there's plenty you could do, Helen. What would you really like to do?"

"I don't know. That's why I was asking for ideas."

"Well, let me think," and her Mum's forehead took on a few more wrinkles while she tried to come up with ideas. "How about looking over some of your schoolwork? That would do you good."

Helen groaned. "Not today, Mum. It's Saturday."

"Your bedroom. You could tidy up your bedroom."

"Mum! No way. That's not fun. I want to do something interesting."

"I know. You could help me. That would be interesting. I was going to clear out all my cupboards and really scrub them down. We could do it together."

"Well, em..." Helen didn't know what to answer. Why had she asked her mother for suggestions? Now she had to find a way of escape from household chores. "Mum, perhaps since the sun is shining, I should go out and get some fresh air. You're always telling me that's what I ought to do."

Mrs Shaw knew what Helen was thinking, and

smiled. When she was eleven she wouldn't have wanted to be stuck indoors with her mother clearing out a kitchen. "Alright. Off you go. I'll manage fine on my own."

Helen didn't hang around in case Mum changed her mind. Within a few minutes she was outside, and making her way down the lane.

It was late March. The morning chill was going, and Helen was glad to be outdoors. The fields looked greener than usual, and the birds seemed to be chirping more loudly than ever. They were enjoying the day.

At the end of the lane, she took the opposite direction to the way she went to school, and headed out into the countryside. On and on she walked, stopping every now and again to look over the fence at cows and sheep. At one point a friendly horse leaned its head over a hedge. Helen pulled some grass, and held it out nervously. Huge teeth emerged and the grass was snatched away. For a moment Helen feared her hand was going with the grass. Before she moved on she counted her fingers to check they were all still there.

Fields of grass gave way to barley, still looking green in the spring sunshine. Up ahead a rabbit was enjoying a meal at the edge of the crop. Usually rabbits stayed hidden during the day, and this one didn't seem to hear Helen approach. 'A deaf rabbit?' she wondered. She kept her footsteps as silent as possible and crept forward, but inevitably the large ears twitched and in a flash the rabbit disappeared down a hole in the grass verge. Helen laughed to herself. 'What a life. Just eat and sleep. That can't be bad.' But when she remembered how many rabbits her biology teacher said died from disease, she decided that being a rabbit was not quite as idyllic as it seemed.

Helen didn't have a watch, so she had no idea how long she'd been out. Time didn't matter very much anyway on a Saturday. But food did! A little while longer, and a few pangs of hunger helped her decide it must be time to head home for lunch.

Back she went, still stopping every now and then to watch a squirrel scampering up a tree or young lambs leaping around in a field. More and more she was growing to love animals. She was so glad she lived near to open countryside.

Eventually she saw familiar hedges and trees. She was nearly home. In the distance were the roofs and chimneys of town, and there was her house down the lane.

As she rounded the last corner, Helen saw a car coming out of town in her direction. That wasn't unusual, but this car stopped near the end of her lane.

'Maybe the driver isn't sure where he's going,' she thought to herself. But, before she could get nearer and help, the passenger door of the car opened, and Helen saw a large polythene bag tossed out. The door slammed shut, the car turned at the end of the lane, and then roared off at great speed back towards town.

'What's going on?' Helen wondered. Then she guessed it. 'Those rotten people - they're dumping their refuse at the end of our lane. I hate when they do that. Why can't they get rid of their rubbish the proper way?'

On she walked the last few yards. Helen grimaced

as she reached the ditch where the people had thrown their garbage. She loved the countryside, and hated people spoiling its beauty. There, tossed into the ditch, was a large, plastic carrier bag. How could they do that? One of her teachers had told her that bags like that hardly decomposed at all. They might still be in the same place in a hundred years time.

'How sad,' Helen thought, and began to walk on towards home.

That's when another thought forced itself to the front of her mind. 'Why not pick up the litter yourself and put it properly into a refuse bin?' Helen groaned. Why did she have to have ideas like that?

'Come on,' the thought persisted. 'Perhaps there isn't much you can do to stop people spoiling the countryside, but you can always help by clearing it up.'

'Okay...,' Helen answered herself. She didn't like picking up someone else's discarded refuse, but she couldn't come to any harm with one carrier bag. Besides, she could see the handles were tied together with string to keep the contents secure, so she wouldn't have to touch whatever was inside.

Helen reached into the ditch, grabbed the bag's handles, and set off up her lane.

She had gone no more than a metre when she felt the bag move. "Eeek!" Helen shrieked. It jerked again. "Yuk! Help!" she screamed, jumping almost off the ground with fright, and dropping the bag on the grass by the edge of the road. She stepped well back from it as quick as she could.

Helen's heart was pounding so hard she could

almost hear it. Every nerve in her body was jangling. She had never had such a bad fright in her life.

It took a couple of minutes before she dared ask herself the obvious question. 'What is in that bag?'

Her mind roamed round the possibilities. 'A rat. A mouse. An injured bird. A not quite dead fish from the lake.' She shuddered. She didn't fancy finding any of those. 'No, this is not my responsibility. I'm leaving the bag where it is, and going home for my lunch.'

With her mind made up, she headed for home as quick as she could. But a dozen steps later she slowed, and turned back. Suppose it really was an injured bird. Probably it was so badly hurt that the people had known it was going to die, and tossed it into the ditch. 'But,' she thought, 'even if it is going to die, they should never have shut it in a bag and abandoned it. I can't just leave it there.'

Reluctantly she bent down to the bag. Whatever was in there was still stirring. She obviously hadn't killed the creature by dropping the bag. There was no choice; she had to help.

Very slowly she reached out for the handles of the carrier bag. Untying the string had to be her first task. It had been wound round and round, before being twisted in unrecognisable knots. Helen was good with her fingers, though, and was managing to undo it fairly easily.

Suddenly the bag lurched sideways. Helen jumped backwards so fast she fell over.

"Ouch," she said as her bottom landed on a sharp stone. But she wasn't really hurt, just scared by the bag.

What was in there?

Back she went to her task, trying to push down the fear she felt churning in her stomach. The last few tangles of string were coming off. Whatever was inside was about to be free.

Helen paused. "What if there is a rat in there?" she asked herself. She knew that rats run away from people, unless they're cornered. That's when they fight, her Dad had told her. And sometimes they bite or claw at the person's throat! She shuddered. She wasn't sure if her Dad had been teasing her or telling the truth. No matter the answer, she didn't fancy meeting a rat face to face.

So she undid the last few strands of string carefully, and stepped away. Whatever was inside could crawl out by itself. She was keeping clear.

Helen watched and waited. Nothing moved. The bag was still. Should she go and open it up?

Before she had to decide, there was more wriggling inside the bag, and she saw brown fur near the opening. She clasped her hand to her mouth. 'It *is* a rat!' She was sure now, and got ready to run.

The brown fur squirmed around some more, and a tiny black nose peeked out from the bag. Above the nose were two little shiny eyes, and a pair of floppy ears.

'A rat...? That's not a rat. It's a... It's a dog!'

Instead of running away, Helen ran towards the bag. The small face of a puppy was looking up at her, and she heard tiny whimpers.

"Poor little thing," Helen said. "You don't want to

be in that bag. Come on out and let me see you."

The puppy wriggled in response, but it couldn't seem to get itself free. Helen reached down carefully, and pulled it from its bag.

Then she saw why it had been struggling. The front and rear paws were both tied with string. 'That's horrible,' Helen thought. 'Whoever put this puppy in here certainly never meant it to get out again.'

"Now just lie still," Helen said soothingly. "I'll soon set you free." It was as if the puppy understood her every word, and did exactly what she said. A few moments later and the string was gone.

The puppy tried to stand, but no sooner was it on its feet than it flopped to the ground again. Helen bent down, and gently picked it up. "Probably your legs are weak because they were tied together. Don't worry. I'll take you home and look after you."

The small dog must have felt safe, because it lay quietly in her arms as she walked the rest of the way up her lane. Helen stroked its head, and spoke softly to comfort it. "You're going to be fine. You're safe now. Nothing bad will ever happen to you again."

Helen's words were slow and careful, but her mind was racing. 'A dog. I've always wanted a dog, and now one has come almost to my doorstep. At last, a puppy who can be mine.'

She reached the side door of her house, and burst in to the kitchen where her Mum was working at the sink.

"Look!" Helen said excitedly. "A dog. It's a dog of my very own."

Chapter 2

Helen's father and mother sipped tea, watching their daughter lovingly stroking the puppy's ears. Her mother's answer to any problem or crisis began with making a pot of tea. It gave her time to think.

Mr Shaw spoke, and he sounded angry: "I read about things like this in the paper. Someone gives their child a puppy for Christmas because it seems a good idea. A few weeks later the novelty of having a pet has worn off, they find out how much work it is to look after an animal, and they simply get rid of it." He shook his head with amazement and sadness. "What a terrible way to do it. How can people tie up a little defenceless dog and throw it in a ditch with almost no air to breathe? If it was up to me, I'd put them in jail for that. Now *we* have to do something with this puppy."

"I've got to keep it," Helen begged. "Besides, it's obvious the previous owners don't want a dog any more."

Her parents both frowned, but it was her mother's turn to speak. "Helen, have you any idea of all that's involved in looking after a dog? It has to be exercised every morning and night. Meals need to be made, and...," she paused, choosing her words carefully, "puppies need someone to constantly clean up the mess they make until they're house trained."

Helen's positive mood wasn't daunted. "I'll do all that. And I'll even enjoy it," she said, a little too enthusiastically.

Her Mum wasn't convinced. "You've never had a dog before. You can't know what it'll be like."

"I know that I've wanted a puppy of my own all my life. I'll learn how to take care of it. I've read books on pets from the library, and I can ask friends who have dogs."

"But who has the work of looking after it while you're out at school? I know who'll get that job," her mother said in a resigned tone.

"I can take Sam out before breakfast... Oh, that's what I've decided to call him, by the way," Helen added. "Then I'll run home at lunchtime to see he's okay. After school I'll come straight back, and I can make his meal before we have ours. That still leaves enough time for walking Sam before bedtime. You see, I can manage it all."

Mrs Shaw looked doubtful. Mr Shaw folded his arms, and shook his head slowly. "The amount of work a dog involves isn't the issue here." His voice sounded serious, and Helen guessed something ominous was coming. "There are two things which matter. One is that we can't afford a dog and the other is that this dog isn't ours to keep."

"What do you mean?" Helen asked anxiously. "I found him, and I know that whoever had him before doesn't want him any more. He meant to kill him." Her eyes filled with tears. "If I hadn't come along Sam wouldn't be alive now. If anyone deserves to have him, it's me."

Her Dad's voice softened. "I understand that, Helen. But you can't simply keep a dog just because you find it. Legally it still belongs to someone else, and, even though it's unlikely, the owner might want it back. This dog is a stray, and since we don't know who it belongs to we'll have to hand it over to the police."

Helen's heart sank. Hopes which had soared sky high earlier were being dashed to the ground. She looked down at the little puppy, sound asleep in her arms. For years she'd wanted a dog just like this. Now she'd found one, only to be told she couldn't keep him. Why did life have to be so cruel?

"Must we call the police, George?" her mother was asking.

"Yes, there's no choice," Mr Shaw replied. "Do you understand that as well, Helen?"

She nodded silently. Her father left, and a moment later Helen heard his distant voice explaining to someone by phone that they had a stray dog. He returned after a few minutes, and said, "A policeman will come round soon."

Helen said nothing, but small tears ran down her cheeks, falling on the puppy's warm body. What had this poor little thing been through until now? How many times had he been shouted at? Had he been hit, or kicked? Some people were so cruel. At last he was safe. At last he was loved. She couldn't lose him. Surely not.

* * * *

Helen sat on the carpet hugging Sam and whispering soothing words in his ear. It wouldn't have required a top class detective to work out that this young girl didn't want to let the puppy go.

The young police officer grimaced. He didn't enjoy this kind of work. "Tell me how you found the puppy," he asked Helen as gently as he could.

"He was in a polythene carrier bag at the end of our lane. He could hardly breathe! It was a horrible way to leave him." Helen's voice grew angry as she spoke. She voiced her father's opinion. "You should put people who do that in jail."

"There are penalties for those who mistreat animals, but it's often hard to catch them doing it. Helen, can you describe the car you saw?"

She struggled to remember, and managed to tell him it was blue, and had four doors, but she had no idea what make of car it was nor what number it had.

The policeman tried to find something positive to say. "You've done well, Helen. But, to be honest, I don't think we're going to find these people, nor does it sound as if they will turn up later to claim the dog."

Helen's face brightened. "Does that mean I can just keep him?"

Her Dad spoke. "It's not as simple as that, Helen."

"That's right," the policeman added. "I'm obliged to take the dog to a special part of the cat and dog home in town, and we must keep him there for a week to see if the owners come for him. If they do, then they can claim him back, although I'd be wanting to ask them some hard questions first."

"What happens if a dog isn't claimed?" asked Mrs Shaw.

"Well, if others have shown interest, they can buy the dog. The cat and dog home don't give animals away, because they must be sure that people are being serious about wanting a pet. I think they charge about £50." He looked down at Helen holding Sam. "Cheer up, you could buy this puppy providing no-one else comes for him."

Helen's father spoke up quickly, "I've told Helen that we can't afford to buy a dog. Finances are already stretched for us."

Helen hung her head, sadness covering her like a cloud. The policeman went to his car for a special basket in which to put Sam. Helen didn't want to let him go, but she realised she had no choice.

"Can I put him in the basket?" she asked.

"Yes, that's no problem," replied the policeman kindly.

She held Sam close for one moment more, then laid him gently inside the basket. She stroked his ears, and smiled bravely at him. "Take care little Sam. I'll never stop thinking about you."

The policeman closed the lid on the basket, and picked it up. "Thank you for all your help. I'll be on my way now."

Very quietly Helen said, "Can I ask you one more question?"

"Yes, Helen, of course you can."

"What will happen to Sam if the owners don't come for him, and no-one offers to buy him?"

The policeman paused. He'd hoped Helen wouldn't ask that question, but since she had she deserved a straight answer. "Helen, the cat and dog home is usually full up. It has no room to keep strays which no-one wants. So, I'm afraid they have to put them down when the time is up."

"You mean that they kill them, don't you?"

"Yes, they do." Helen's brutal honesty had made the policemen feel even more uncomfortable. "They have no choice. Perhaps they won't need to do that in this case," he added, hoping to cheer her up.

But nothing could cheer Helen up now. She stood at the door of her house watching the police car disappearing up the lane, and tear after tear flowed down her cheeks. She had never felt so sad in all her life.

* * * *

It was bedtime, though Helen was in no mood for sleep. Her mind was still full of all that had happened earlier in the day. She relived her walk. She could 'see' the car come along the road, the door open and a bag thrown out. She could picture herself almost leaving the bag where it was, but going back for it and so carefully undoing its string. She felt both the terror and the joy of finding what it contained.

Helen lay across her bed. Over and over the sequence of events and emotions ran through her mind. She tried to change the last part of the story, and imagine that she was still holding Sam, hers for ever. But no amount of wishful thinking could change the ending. The 'replay' was always the same: she heard her father say they couldn't afford a dog, and then the policeman came to take Sam away.

She hated that part. She didn't blame the policeman. He was only doing his job. She was tempted to blame her father. Why couldn't he have said that they'd buy Sam if the owners didn't claim him? She knew the people who had dumped him in the ditch would never come back for him, so Sam would have been hers in a week's time. Yet, how could she say it was her Dad's fault? If he couldn't buy even a paper, how could he agree to spending £50 on a dog?

Helen lay in the darkness wishing lots of things. She wished her father had as much money as Wendy's father. She wished she had money of her own. She wished she had a rich aunt who would send her money. But her Dad had nothing, she had nothing, and her one great aunt wasn't wealthy and never sent her anything. It was hopeless. Sam would never be hers.

Time dragged past. Helen eventually gave up her dreaming and decided she would have to go to bed.

The last thing she did every night was pray. Too often she rushed through a list of things, or said the same prayer each night. But this night there was only one thing on her mind. Usually she just lay on her back to pray, but she felt so much that she wanted to pour out her heart to God that she knelt by the side of the bed.

"God, dear God," she prayed, "I don't understand how you allowed me to find little Sam only to have him taken away again and maybe put to death next week. You know how long I've wanted a dog of my own, and one just like Sam would be wonderful." Helen paused.

She was never quite sure how directly she should speak to God. She'd always been taught to show respect to God, but she couldn't help telling him all that was on her heart. "God, I've just got to ask you this. If there's any way at all that Sam could be mine, would you please make that happen? I can't think of any way, because we haven't any money. But I've always believed you can do anything at all. So, please help…"

Her voice trailed off. No more words seemed to come. Her bones began to ache, and she realised how tired she felt. All that had happened on that supposedly empty Saturday had made her exhausted. She pulled back the covers of her bed, and climbed in.

Her head had hardly touched the pillow when the most impossible of thoughts came into her mind. Lying there in the darkness, she suddenly knew that she would have Sam as her very own. It was as if someone was writing across her mind in large letters: 'Sam will be yours'. And the someone was God! She had never been more certain of anything. She blinked her eyes and shook her head to make sure she was still awake. But she was, and the message in her mind was unchanged. How Sam would become hers, she had no idea. But he would. She knew he would. It was God's answer.

Within two minutes she was sound asleep, a quiet smile lingering on her face.

Chapter 3

Morning came, and Helen woke feeling still tired. She'd tossed and turned all night, never able to sleep properly. Her body had been weary enough, but her mind had been racing at 100 miles per hour, reliving and reviewing all that had happened during Saturday.

Sunday meant church for Helen and her parents. Helen didn't mind that. In fact she usually enjoyed it. None of her friends ever went, but Helen had always been taught that she should do what was right no matter what anyone else thought or did.

This morning she seemed to have so little energy, and set a new personal record for slow speed in getting dressed and ready. Later she ate breakfast with her parents, but no-one talked very much.

Church was probably much the same as usual, and any other week Helen would have been happy to be there. But not today. She couldn't concentrate on what was being said when her thoughts kept going back to a little puppy called Sam. How was he feeling, probably lying in a cage in the cat and dog home? He must be so lonely. Did he miss her? She certainly missed him.

Church service over, and she waited for her parents to finish all their conversations. Why did they always

talk so much? How did church people find so much to
say? She was sure they could have Sunday lunch at least
half-an-hour earlier if only they could leave church as
soon as the service finished.

Her thoughts were startled by a cheerful voice from
behind. "Hello Helen. How are you today?"

She whirled round. It was Miss Williams. She used
to be her Sunday School teacher, and Helen had always
liked her. "I'm fine, mostly," she replied.

"Mostly? Now, does that mean you're really not so
fine?" Miss Williams was smiling, but she was asking
seriously.

"No, I'm okay. It's just…" Helen paused. Should
she tell her about Sam? Why not? At least Miss
Williams could be trusted not to think she was being
stupid. "Well, I found a little puppy yesterday which
had been abandoned, and I brought him home and called
him Sam. I wanted to keep him, but Mum and Dad
wouldn't let me."

"They wouldn't let you? Is that the whole story?"

"No, I suppose not. They told me the police had to
be called, and the policeman who came round said the
owners might want their dog back. He took Sam away
meantime to the cat and dog home."

"So, your parents aren't really to blame, are they?"
Miss Williams had always forced her to be honest.

"No, you're right. The real problem is that they
don't seem to think there's any way we can afford to buy
back this puppy from the home, and if no-one does after
a week he'll be killed. That's terrible!" Helen turned
her head away. She could feel the tears beginning to

come again, and she didn't want to cry in front of her former Sunday School teacher.

"Helen, parents often have many, many expenses and financial responsibilities. There are probably a lot of things they'd like to have too, but they can't because there isn't money for everything."

Helen decided to take a big risk. "I understand that," she said, "but last night, just after I prayed, I felt deep inside that I was meant to have this puppy as my own."

"How did you know that?"

"I can't explain. I just knew."

"Have you told your parents that part?"

"No, not yet."

"Wouldn't that be the right thing to do, Helen? I'm sure they'll listen to what you say."

"Maybe. But at the end of it all, there'll still be the fact that the cat and dog home won't part with a pet unless the new owner pays £50. And I know my Mum and Dad can't afford that."

"At least tell them what you're thinking. That's always good."

"Okay, I'll try."

Miss Williams looked at her watch. "I've got to run Helen. I've some friends coming for lunch, and I've still all the potatoes to peel!" Helen smiled. Miss Williams was a lovely person, but she was nearly always late! Helen wouldn't be surprised if the guests were queuing at the door waiting to get in.

"Thanks for taking time to talk to me," Helen said.

Miss Williams was already walking down the driveway from the church. "That's a pleasure," she called over her shoulder. "I'll certainly be praying about your little Sam. Don't give up hope. That deep feeling inside you last night might be very important."

"I hope so. I really hope so," Helen muttered as she watched her older friend disappearing.

* * * *

Helen's parents talked about a whole catalogue of things during Sunday lunch. First there was the weather. Would it rain today, or would the sun stay out long enough for them to have a walk later in the afternoon? They concluded that an outing might be worth the risk if they had enough energy left after lunch.

Then they debated the sermon they'd heard at church. This was a regular topic, and Helen called it 'having roast preacher for lunch'. At least that day they considered what they had heard was interesting and challenging. 'Most unusual,' thought Helen, but kept quiet in case they asked her opinion, and by now she couldn't even remember what the sermon was about.

They did bring Helen into the conversation, however, when they moved to the next subject. "What has Wendy been doing this weekend?" her mother asked.

"She's been away at a hotel with her family."

"At a hotel? That must be costing her father a lot of money," said Mr Shaw.

"Wendy says he's just had another bonus, so he's spending some of it on a family treat."

Her Dad grimaced. "I wouldn't mind the chance to do that."

"Never mind George," Helen's Mum said quickly.

"We have plenty to be thankful for. There are many things in life more important than money."

Helen's spirits sank lower. This line of conversation wasn't helping what she wanted to talk about with her parents. She sat listening for a few more minutes, working up her courage. Then her moment came. "Mum, Dad, can I tell you something?"

Her mother exchanged an anxious look with her father. "Of course, Helen, tell us what's on your mind."

"It's about Sam."

"Oh... Well, I'm sure he's alright in the cat and dog home." Mrs Shaw was using her most reassuring tone of voice.

"Perhaps," Helen replied, "but only for a week. After that he doesn't get to live."

"Perhaps his owners will have second thoughts, and collect him."

"Mum, I'm eleven. I may not be grown up yet, but I'm certainly old enough to know there's very little chance of that happening."

"Helen," Mr Shaw said, "if this conversation is leading up to asking us to buy this puppy for you, then you should know that what I said yesterday is still true. We simply haven't got £50 to spend on a dog."

"Dad, isn't there some way? Surely £50 isn't impossible?"

Her father got up, and walked over to a cabinet. He pulled open the top drawer, and took out a handful of brown envelopes. "Helen, these are all bills which have to be paid in the next few weeks." He leafed through them as he spoke. "This one is for £60 - that's for electricity. The next is a payment due on the car. It's £150. Here's our mortgage statement, now £200. Do you remember how we had to have our roof mended after the rain started coming in?" Helen nodded. "Well here's the bill for that repair, and it's £500. And there's more, for your piano lessons, servicing costs for the car, house insurance, and others. That's not to mention the money we believe it's right to give to God as our church offerings. Add it all together, and right now we are due payments of well over a thousand pounds." Helen's face looked more glum than ever.

"So, Helen, that's why there isn't £50 to spare at the moment. We simply haven't got that money."

"Is this a specially bad time?" Helen asked.

Mr Shaw sighed. "Yes and no. It is particularly tough at the moment, but the truth is that there's never been a time for many years when finding enough money hasn't been a struggle."

Looking across at her father, Helen suddenly felt very sorry for him. She had always known they weren't well off, but she had never realised just how difficult it was every month to make ends meet. Yet her Dad never complained. Even now, he was telling her these problems only to help her understand.

Helen didn't know what to do now. To talk any more about Sam seemed so selfish. Yet, something inside her couldn't give up on this little puppy. She had to tell her parents what she felt.

"Dad, thank you for telling me how things really are about our money. I don't want to upset you and Mum, but can I tell you how I feel inside?"

"We want to know, Helen. Go ahead," said her mother.

"Well, I was praying about the puppy." She reckoned it never did any harm to introduce a spiritual note. "After I'd finished, I felt so sad that Sam had been taken away. It hurt badly inside to think that he would die in a week's time."

Helen glanced at her parents. Her Mum and Dad were listening intently. "Go on," her father said.

"Then it changed. I mean my mood did. I became sure - really sure - that Sam wouldn't die, and that he would become my very own puppy. I knew that's what God was saying. Couldn't that be right?"

Her Dad sat back in his chair, a thoughtful look on his face. He didn't usually speak quickly at times like these. Her Mum did though. "Oh Helen, how could you know that what you felt wasn't just your wishful thinking?"

"Of course it is what I want. But last night there seemed no way at all that Sam could be mine. So, if anything, my feelings should have stayed stuck with the likelihood that he'd never come out of the cat and dog home."

"Helen, your father has just shown you how difficult money is for us at the moment. Can't you see that?"

"I do see it. But I also felt sure that somehow Sam would be mine. I really believe that, even today."

There was silence for what seemed like an age. Everyone was thinking. Eventually, Mr Shaw leaned forward and spoke. "Alright Helen, I'm prepared to take what you say seriously, in the sense that I accept you really thought God was telling you that the puppy would be yours."

Helen brightened. This sounded a little more positive than anything before.

Her Dad went on, "What I can't believe, though, is that God would want us to spend £50 on a dog when that £50 is already owed to other people. That couldn't be right. In a sense, it would be like stealing." He paused, and Helen wondered what could be coming next. The situation had sounded hopeful, and in a second had become hopeless again.

She didn't have to wait long. "So," her father continued, "if God means Sam to be yours, and if he will cost £50, then God will have to provide a new £50 to buy him. What's more, I believe he'll have to put that £50 in your hands, not mine. Finally, to make sure God really is behind this, you mustn't go rushing around trying to make the money by doing odd jobs. This has to be money we know has come from God."

"But that's impossible," Helen protested. "I never have any money of my own, never mind £50. What's more, I'd have to have the money in the next week or it'll be too late for Sam. There's no way at all that can happen."

"Helen, do you believe God told you?"

"Yes, but..."

"And do you believe that God can do even the impossible?" her Dad persisted.

"Well... Yes..." Poor Helen was lost for any words that sounded sensible.

Her father spoke softly now. "Helen, let's leave it like this for the moment. I know as well as you how hard it'll be for you to get £50 in the next week. So, if it comes, that must be from God, and we'll be meant to have that puppy, and I'll accept the cost which will come long term for feeding it and other expenses. You must accept, though, that if there's no new money to buy this puppy, then God didn't really tell you that you were to have him. Can you do that, Helen?"

Helen sank back in her seat, feeling powerless. If she could have thought of any other way forward than this, she'd have argued for it. But her mind was a blank. What her father had proposed was the only possibility.

"Alright," she said, "I accept. But I'm going to have to do an awful lot of praying this week."

All three smiled at that. "We'll do that too," her Mum said, "and it will do every one of us good."

Chapter 4

"Hi! Do you want to hear about my fabulous weekend?" Wendy was bouncing with excitement when Helen met her on the way to school next morning, and didn't wait for an answer to her question. "It was fantastic. I spent the whole weekend living in luxury. I don't think I could have had a better time."

Helen smiled. Wendy enthused about most things, but even by the 'Wendy standard' this time away must have been really good.

"There was a thirty metre swimming pool which was really warm, a jacuzzi nearby where you could lie back and soak in the bubbles. The sauna was roasting - I thought I was turning into a beetroot. Then there was a fitness room with special cycles, running tracks, weights, and exercise benches. I would be pounds lighter if there hadn't been gargantuan meals. Outside was even better. I'm not boring you, am I?"

"Oh no," Helen said in a resigned tone.

"Good. Well, there were tennis courts, a putting green, a golf course, and even horse riding. Over in another building were the badminton and squash courts, and a trampoline. I tell you, Helen, I hardly stopped from morning to night."

"It doesn't sound like you did."

"And what do you think of my hair? Isn't it fabulous?" Helen had noticed the new style and had meant to comment, but hadn't had a chance. On Wendy went, "The hotel had its own hairdressing salon, and a hair beautician - that's what they call their hairdressers - gave me what he called 'a unique cut designed to bring out the best in my hair'. And yes, he was male, a real dishy guy called Kevin. I loved it - and him!"

"Was there anything not perfect?" asked Helen.

"I don't think so. Even Dad was in a good mood. No, the only bad part of the whole weekend was leaving to come back last night, and then to school this morning." Wendy wrinkled her nose. "I don't suppose anybody can live like that all the time. But it would be nice!"

By now they were at the school gates. Wendy had hardly got started on describing her 'palatial hotel bedroom' when the bell was ringing. Since the two girls were in different registration classes, they had to separate.

"I'll see you at morning break," Wendy said. "I'll tell you more then what it was like and all I did." She paused, then added, "And you can tell me if anything exciting happened to you." Then, with a wave, she was off.

'Typical Wendy,' thought Helen, who really liked her friend. 'She's always full of what she's been doing, but at least she doesn't completely forget about others.'

Helen didn't find it easy to concentrate during the first lessons of the day. Any time a teacher was even a little boring - and that morning most of them seemed very boring indeed - her mind slipped into thinking about Sam. 'How was he now? Was he eating his food? How much space did he have? Was he in a cage with other dogs? If the dogs fought, how would Sam survive since he was so small? And what was going to happen to him eventually? Could he ever be hers?' Those last two questions went round and round in her mind more than any of the others.

She tried to get her thoughts back on a schoolwork track. But maths was terribly dull on a Monday morning. She was fighting a losing battle with her interest. Why couldn't they have lessons on how to look after pets?

Finally 11.00 a.m. came and they had a fifteen minute break. She found Wendy heading for the girls' toilets, the place many of them went for a chat.

"So the food was good at the hotel…?" said Helen, giving Wendy an opening to talk some more about her weekend away.

Off Wendy went again, giving detail upon detail of the luxury in which she'd lived. Helen was tolerant, and smiled and nodded at all the right moments.

The long narrative of experiences and emotions eventually slowed. It was more a pause than an ending, Helen guessed, while Wendy chose which part of her mini holiday to relate next.

But she didn't. Instead she asked, "Now, before I go on, tell me if your weekend was as dull as you thought it would be."

"No, I wouldn't have said it turned out dull.

Actually, it was quite eventful."

"Really! Tell me!" Wendy sounded excited. "Did you meet a boy...?" she teased.

"Hmm, I did meet someone... His name was Sam," said Helen.

"What! You did meet a boy?! Wow! What was he like? Was he tall?"

"Sam was a little on the short side, but that didn't seem to matter to us."

"I agree," said Wendy, as if she was an authority on the opposite sex. "What colour was his hair?"

"Mostly a gentle brown, I'd say, and his eyes matched. Quite dreamy really."

Wendy gave a pleasurable shudder. She'd already conjured up a mental image of this gorgeous young man Helen had met. "And what did you do?"

"Well, we spent quite a bit of time on Saturday just cuddled up together."

Wendy's eyes rolled. And right at that moment the bell sounded for classes to resume.

"I'm off to French," said Helen. "I'll see you at lunchtime. Perhaps I'll tell you a little more about Sam then."

"You'd better," Wendy shouted after her, looking dazed.

Helen headed off for her French class, feeling a little guilty, but laughing inside. Poor Wendy didn't know any longer which one of them had had the better weekend.

* * * *

"You rotter! You cheat! You deceiver!" Wendy's words sounded harsh but she was smiling as she spoke. It was lunchtime, and the friends were seated on a wall at the side of the playground, eating their sandwiches.

"All I said was that his name was Sam, and the description of him I gave was true. It was you who added two and two and made five."

"Yes, but you let me believe you'd found some fantastic guy. And to think I was getting excited for you..." Wendy sounded disappointed, but Helen guessed she might not have been all that enthusiastic if she had really had a boyfriend while Wendy didn't.

"I was excited to have found a dog," Helen went on.

"I believe you. I know how often you've talked about that in the past. Getting Sam must be like a dream come true."

Helen had not had a chance to tell Wendy the whole story. "It was a dream which turned into a nightmare," she said quietly and seriously.

"Hmm? What does that mean?"

"Since the puppy was abandoned, I can't just keep it. My Dad called the police who have put Sam into care for one week. After that, we could buy him for £50, but that's not possible."

"Not possible? It sounds straightforward to me."

"It would be for most people, but - and don't let on that I've told you this - we simply can't afford £50 at the moment. We've too many other things to pay for."

"So, if you don't buy him, what will happen to Sam?"

"The owner could claim him, though no-one expects

that to happen since he dumped him in the first place. It's also possible for someone else to buy Sam, but that's not likely either. My Dad says the cat and dog home always has too many dogs."

"So, if the owner doesn't get him back, and neither you nor anyone else buys him, what'll happen to Sam?"

There was a long pause. Eventually Helen answered softly, "They'll kill him."

"Kill him? Why?"

"Because they can't go on feeding abandoned dogs which no-one wants."

"How will they do it?"

"I don't know. I was wondering about that myself last night. I must try and find out."

"However they do it, that's horrible," said Wendy. "Is there no other possibility?"

"There doesn't seem to be."

"When will they do it, I mean, when will they kill him?" Wendy was asking a lot of questions. She was feeling as horrified as Helen about a little puppy having to die.

"The policeman said there would be a week for the owner to claim his dog, or for someone else to offer to buy him. That takes us to next Saturday. Dad says they wouldn't put a dog to death at a weekend, so next Monday will be the day."

"Next Monday is a school holiday..." Wendy mused. Her mind had gone off on a sidetrack. "Hey! It's also your birthday!"

"My birthday?" Helen did some rapid calculating of dates. "So it is. I'd forgotten all about it." Then her face fell. "I hate the thought that Sam might die on my birthday."

"That does sound tough."

Helen brightened. "Don't worry. It'll be a good day because I don't believe Sam will die."

"That sounds like extreme optimism to me."

"I mean it."

"How can you know?"

"That's hard to explain."

"Try me."

Helen groaned inside. How do you describe in believable terms that you think God told you something? And how do you do that when the person you're telling doesn't go to church and doesn't seem to believe much about God? Wendy, best friend that she was, might think she'd gone crazy. But Helen had to say something now.

"All I can tell you is that I got a strange inner feeling about it."

"How? When? What kind of feeling?" Wendy could be very persistent at times.

"I can't describe it precisely," said Helen. Then she worked up all her courage. "It came after I'd been praying."

"After you'd what?!"

Wendy's question exploded with surprise. It seemed Helen might as well have said she'd been talking with a little green man from Mars.

"I had been praying to God, and at the end of it I just knew that God was going to let me have this little puppy for myself."

Wendy looked absolutely stunned. "I didn't know what you were going to say, but I certainly didn't expect this. Have you been feeling unwell? Is all the excitement of the weekend getting to you?"

"I'm fine, and I meant everything I said."

"Well, I wouldn't tell too many others, if I were you. They'll think a whole load of screws have come loose up top."

"I wasn't planning to tell them, because there's no need. I only told you because you're my best friend, and because you asked."

"Did you let your parents know?"

"Yes, I thought that was the right thing to do."

"What did they say?"

"They were okay about it. They said they would accept what I said was right, and that we were meant to have the puppy, if £50 comes this week."

"What do you mean 'comes'?"

"I'm not sure. Before the week is over I must have £50, but I don't know at the moment how I'm going to get it. I'll have to keep praying."

"Wow! Do you mean you can get £50 just by praying? I must take it up!"

"It's not like that, and you know it. The money will come only if it's right for me to keep Sam, and I believe it is. So, somehow that money will be there by the time I need it."

Wendy sat for a while gazing out over the playground. Helen sat quietly too, realising she'd let Wendy see some of the important things in her life more clearly than she'd ever done before. That scared her. Anyone less than the best of friends might make fun of her for what she believed.

After a while, Wendy said, "Helen, I don't want Sam to die either. I'd like to help you save him."

"How can you do that?"

"I'll speak to my Dad about it, and tell him I need £50 to help you buy him from the cat and dog home."

"You can't do that! Don't think I'm not grateful, but it's not your Dad's problem. It's mine."

"Nonsense. Wait and see what I can do."

Lunchtime was over, and classes were about to start. Both girls climbed down from their perches on the wall, and made their way towards the classrooms.

Helen's mind was whirring. Wendy's Dad certainly didn't have the same kind of money problems as her father. He probably carried £50 notes around in his pocket for everyday expenses. But was it right that he should be involved in all this? Was he to be the answer to her prayer, and so quickly?

"When will you talk to him about it Wendy?" asked Helen just before they parted.

"I'll do it tonight. There's no reason for any delay!"

Wendy was back to her bouncy, enthusiastic self. As far as she was concerned, the problems about Sam were as good as over. Helen couldn't quite manage the same confidence. But she hoped - lots.

Chapter 5

Next morning Helen set off for school with mixed emotions. She couldn't ignore Wendy's super-confidence that her Dad would immediately come up with £50, guaranteeing that she would have Sam for herself at the end of the week. Her heart pounded with quiet excitement at the possibility.

Yet…could it really be that easy? It seemed too good to be true that the money she needed would come so quickly. Wendy's Dad wasn't likely to be impressed by the idea that God would provide by means of him donating £50.

As she walked, her mind tossed the arguments back and forward. She'd been doing it ever since the previous day's conversation. One line of logic said there was no reason why God shouldn't answer prayer quickly, and there were plenty of examples in the Bible of God using some very strange people for his purposes. So why not Wendy's father? The other line of logic said Wendy couldn't speak for her father, and he might have very different ideas of what he wanted to do with £50.

Along her lane she went, and down the road towards town. Away up ahead she saw Wendy waiting at the usual corner. Her heart beat a little faster. She was about to find out whether she would have a puppy, and whether Sam would live or die.

Helen knew the answer even before she met Wendy. Normally her friend was bouncing with news and full of life. But not today. Her head hung low, and there wasn't a single smile for Helen as she came near.

"I don't know how to explain..." Wendy began.

"Your Dad didn't want to give £50," Helen helped her out.

"I'm sorry."

"That's alright. I shouldn't have allowed myself to believe it was ever likely."

"It's not that he didn't feel sorry for Sam," Wendy tried to explain. "He listened very carefully to everything I told him, but then he said it wasn't his place to interfere. The decision about whether or not you should have a dog was only for you and your family. I tried to change his mind, but my Dad never changes his mind." Wendy looked more depressed than ever.

"Don't worry, it's not your fault. I know you tried your best to help me." Helen gave Wendy a quick hug of encouragement.

"I'm the one who's supposed to cheer you up in your disappointment," Wendy said ruefully.

Helen managed to laugh. "I'll be okay. After all, I'm not any worse off than I was before you made your offer yesterday."

"You are in the sense that there's now one less way to save Sam."

"Okay, you're right, but since I never could think of

any way in which this money could come, I'm not sure that makes much difference."

Wendy gave Helen an admiring look. "You are very brave! I don't think I could be as calm as you."

On they walked towards school, with Helen wondering how she could look so calm when she felt so hurt and sad inside.

* * * *

Another day had passed. Now it was Wednesday, and school was over for the day. Helen and Wendy walked down the road, chatting much as usual.

"Dad's off on another business trip," said Wendy.

"How long will he be away this time?"

"Not long, thankfully. He said he'd be back for the weekend."

"How does your mother manage without him? I don't think my Mum would like it if Dad was away from home often."

"She used to be frightened. I don't think she liked being alone late at night, in case there were any burglars lurking around. But she doesn't think about that any more. She told me she keeps a wooden mallet under the bed to deal with any intruders. She would use it too!"

"My Mum would just scream. That would probably scare most burglars off as well. For the moment, though, she says she'll just send Dad off to investigate any suspicious noises. That's what husbands are for." They both laughed.

They walked on, winding their way through the streets. Wendy had an unusual moment of silence, while she was thinking. "Maybe if your father got a job which made him go away every now and then, your parents could be persuaded to get a dog to help your Mum feel safe."

Helen shook her head. "No chance. Even though my Dad doesn't get paid very much, he enjoys what he does, and he says that job security is very important. He'd never change."

"It would solve your problem about getting a dog if he did, though."

"Not really," Helen replied, "because I believe Sam is the puppy I'm meant to have, and even if he wanted to my Dad couldn't change jobs before Monday."

"I suppose not," Wendy agreed.

By now they'd reached the corner where they parted. "I'm not going straight home," Helen said. "I'm going into the middle of town to the library."

Wendy raised her eyebrows questioningly. "You don't usually do things like that," she said. "You must have become extra keen on reading."

"I have to do a little research about something," Helen replied mysteriously. "I'd rather not go into detail."

"I bet you're off to research some good looking lad, and you've arranged to meet romantically between the bookshelves."

Helen smiled. "You'll just have to wonder and imagine, Wendy. But don't get too jealous."

They walked on a little further, and then reached a road junction where Wendy had to turn right towards her house. "Have a good time at the library," she called back to Helen as she headed home.

"I'll try," Helen shouted. "See you tomorrow."

Helen walked for another fifteen minutes to the main street where the library was located. For the size of her town it was a large building, with books on two different storeys. The ground level was usually the busiest, because that was where people went to borrow books they wanted to take home and read. But Helen climbed the stairs to the first floor, to what was called the reference department. They kept all the biggest books there such as dictionaries and encyclopaedias. No-one could take these books away, but people were welcome to look up any information they wanted.

Helen hadn't often been to that part of the library before. She wasn't sure where to start. An attentive librarian came to her rescue. Leaning over from behind her large desk, she asked, "Can I help you?"

"Yes, can you tell me where to find books about dogs?" Helen's voice was a polite whisper. She'd seen a dozen or so people deeply engrossed in books, and didn't want to disturb them.

"Certainly. If you go to the fourth set of shelves on the right hand side, you'll see a whole category of books about pets, and one section of that is on dogs. Probably you'll find something suitable there."

"Thank you," Helen replied, impressed with the librarian's efficiency.

She moved down the rows of books, and easily found the correct one. She had no problem either with tracing the section on dogs, since it was by far the largest. Helen's eyes bulged as she scanned the rows.

There seemed to be a book on just about every breed of dog, and there were a lot of breeds!

None of these were what Helen wanted though. She needed a different kind of information. "Let's see…" she murmured to herself as she studied the titles further along the shelf. There were books on training dogs, breeding dogs, dogs for the blind, dog illnesses, famous dogs in history. 'There can't be many more books on dogs which can be written,' she thought.

Then, at last, her eyes spotted a book which might help her. Its title was, *Stray Dogs*. Helen pulled it off the shelf, and moved over to one of the large tables where she could read the book properly.

She opened it up at the contents page to look at the chapter titles. They seemed to cover a wide range: which people allowed their dogs to roam, why people abandon dogs completely, which types of dogs were most often made into strays, diseases stray dogs might have, and the care given to strays in homes. Right at the end was a chapter called, 'When all fails'. She turned up the page and began to read.

The author talked about how hard all cat and dog homes tried to find owners for abandoned pets. Often they succeeded, but when they didn't their only option was to put the dogs to death. Helen's eyes skimmed down the page, taking in the words as fast as she could. What she wanted to know was simply how the dogs died.

At last she found the paragraph which told her. She read, and she cried. Big tears ran down her cheeks, and dropped on the page of the book. She had to reach into her pocket quickly for a paper handkerchief, wipe the page clean and catch more tears. Thankfully no-one else seemed to have noticed that she was crying.

When she had calmed down enough, she took out a small notebook from her school case, and wrote down what the book said.

Half an hour later she was home. Her mother was busy making the evening meal, and Helen perched on a stool in the kitchen. "It's horrible," she said.

"What is?" asked her mother, hoping Helen wasn't describing the food she was preparing.

"The way they kill dogs in a home."

"Is that what you went to the library to find out?"

"Yes, and I almost wish I hadn't." She pulled out her notebook. "Let me tell you what the book said."

Helen began to read. "The most commonly used method is electrocution. The dog is placed in what is known as a Hulec Chamber and electrodes (wires to carry electricity) are attached to ears and feet. Then the operator switches on a powerful electric current for approximately thirty seconds..."

Poor Helen couldn't stop the tears coming again. Her mother wiped her hands on a towel, and put her arms round Helen. "It's alright, Helen. Don't be upset. I'm sure the dogs don't feel any pain at all. It must all be over instantly."

"I know that," Helen sobbed. "It's just that I can't bear the thought of little Sam dying like that."

"Are you sure that's how they do it in our cat and dog home?"

"Well, the book said the biggest homes are changing.

Many now inject huge doses of anaesthetic which put the dog to sleep before stopping its heart. It's the small homes which are still doing it the old way. Our home isn't big at all…" Her words ran out, and she cried and cried.

A moment later, and she felt warm drops on the top of her head. Her Mum was crying as much as she was.

Chapter 6

Thursday seemed a very long and sad day for Helen. Her lessons dragged. There was never very much about maths and chemistry to excite Helen, but that day they seemed worse than ever. Normally the English class interested her, but it was as dull as all the rest.

She knew the real problem had nothing to do with her school lessons. Helen was depressed because the week was rapidly going past and she wasn't one penny nearer to having any money to rescue Sam. Since even small amounts of money never came her way unexpectedly, right from the first mention on Sunday afternoon she'd found it hard to believe that £50 could materialise. Yet, she was so sure God meant her to have Sam that something must happen to make that possible. But now it was Thursday. Sam probably had only three more full days to live.

'If only there were something to encourage me,' she thought. 'Just something to help me believe Sam could be saved.' But there was nothing. Wendy's optimism had died. Her parents never talked about Sam unless she raised the subject. Her Mum was keeping herself busy in the kitchen, and her Dad wasn't around to talk to. He'd begun to do some work in his garden shed in the evenings. 'Probably keeping out of my way,' reflected Helen a little unkindly.

So it was a weary Helen who trudged home from school that afternoon. Wendy had chattered away much as usual on the way down the road. Helen didn't mind as long as all she had to do was nod occasionally to indicate she was listening. But her mind was really on a little puppy locked in a home.

She made her way up the lane, and into her house. "I'm home Mum," she called.

"Hello!" her Mum shouted back from the kitchen. "How was your day?"

"Don't ask."

"Oh. It was like that?"

"Yes it was. Mum, what's going to happen to Sam?"

"I don't know that any more than you do Helen. Mind you, I did make one phone call today which you might be interested in."

Helen raised her eyebrows questioningly.

"I phoned the cat and dog home. I wondered if perhaps the owner had collected his puppy, or if someone else had offered to buy him. Either of those would have meant there was no point in you continuing to be so anxious about him."

"And...?" Helen asked, more anxious than ever. She wasn't sure what would be good news and bad news right now. If Sam had been collected, or someone else wanted to buy him, he would be saved. But then he would never be hers! She didn't want him to die, but neither did she want anyone else to have him.

Her Mum had already anticipated Helen's reaction.

"It's alright. Apparently there's been no interest at all in Sam."

Helen sighed with relief, though she felt guilty at her own selfishness. Yet, was she just being selfish at wanting a dog of her own, or did she really believe Sam was meant to be hers? Helen herself didn't fully know the answer to that question.

Mrs Shaw poured out a cup of tea for her, and they sat together at the kitchen table. "Suppose nothing happens by the weekend. Do you think Dad will change his mind?"

"Helen, your Dad isn't in a position to change his mind. He told you what our family finances are like at the moment."

"But if we get right to next Monday, how can we simply sit here knowing that Sam is being put to death?" Helen's voice was filled with sadness. "I don't know if I could cope with that."

"Helen, you may have to. There are times when things happen which we hate, and there's nothing at all we can do to change them."

"But, Mum, we're Christians, and you've always taught me that God loves us and that he can do anything he wants. So, surely he wouldn't simply let a harmless little puppy die because no-one either wanted him or could afford him?"

Her Mum sat silent for a moment. Why did her daughter have to ask questions like this? "Helen, I don't know how to answer that. All I can say is that this world isn't the perfect place God made it originally. People do all sorts of wrong things, and they've spoiled it. So bad things happen which God never meant. One day it won't be like that, but by then we'll be in heaven."

"That'll be a bit late for Sam," Helen said in a disappointed tone of voice.

"Oh, by the way, I forgot to mention that a letter came for you today." Her Mum was glad to be able to change the subject. "Now, where is it...? I put it somewhere safe." That was usually fatal. Sometimes Mrs Shaw made things so safe no-one could find them again, including her. She moved through to the next room to see if she'd put it in a drawer.

'Who could be writing to me?' Helen wondered. She didn't usually get any letters. When her Mum hadn't reappeared after five minutes, Helen went through to help her search.

They scoured the room for the envelope, looking behind cushions, on window ledges, in drawers - anywhere they could think of. Mrs Shaw was getting a little anxious. "I'm sure we'll find it eventually, Helen," she said, standing in the middle of the room scratching her head. Her gaze wandered round the room. "There it is!" she announced triumphantly as she stared at the wall in front of her. "I tucked the envelope into the picture frame because I knew someone must look at it eventually."

She pulled it from the frame, and handed it to Helen. "I'm so glad we found it."

So was Helen, wanting to know who it had come from. She scrutinised the envelope but didn't recognise the handwriting.

There was one sure way to find out who was writing to her. Helen tore open the envelope, and pulled out the letter inside. As she read, her eyes opened wider with each line.

Dear Helen,

I thought a lot about our conversation after church on Sunday concerning the little puppy you found, and what you told me you believed should happen. As you know, I promised to pray about the whole matter.

At first, I wondered if you were simply engaging in wishful thinking, but the more I have prayed the more I have come to share your belief about Sam. In addition, I felt God wanted me to help just a little towards the sum you need to buy this puppy, so with this letter you'll find a £10 note.

Now I'll keep praying that you get the rest of the money for Sam.

Your friend,
Margaret Williams.

When she'd pulled out the letter, Helen had crumpled the envelope in her hand. As she finished reading, she straightened it out again, and looked inside. Sure enough, there was the £10 note.

"Mum!" Helen said incredulously, "I've got £10 towards Sam. It's from Miss Williams. She thinks God wants me to have him." Her eyes sparkled. Thursday wasn't such a bad day after all.

"That's marvellous!" her Mum said. "Can I read her letter?"

"Of course." Helen handed it over.

"Well, she sounds about as sure as you, doesn't she?" commented her Mum when she'd finished reading. "Isn't that good?"

Helen nodded enthusiastically. "Maybe I should talk to more people about Sam, and then they might give contributions as well!"

"No, that wouldn't be right, Helen. That way you'd be trying to create the miracle you need, instead of allowing God to do it his way. You can't organise God."

"Can't I?" Helen asked, pouting her bottom lip, but she was only teasing.

"If God means you to have Sam, then he can bring the rest that's needed in ways you could never arrange anyway."

Helen frowned again. "But there's still £40 to go."

"Don't look at it that way. Give thanks for the £10 you've got already."

Her Mum was right, and Helen gave her a big hug. And, as they stood there, both breathed a short prayer of thanks to God for the money which had come, Helen adding a little request for what was yet to come.

Chapter 7

Helen went to sleep that night feeling encouraged. She had believed since the previous Saturday that Sam would somehow be hers. But until today, belief was all she had. There had been nothing to back up her faith. Now there was something, a very real £10. She slept well.

Friday morning dawned with dark clouds scudding across the sky. Helen felt like the sky looked. The lightness she'd sensed in her heart the previous night was gone, and her mood was much more sombre. It took all her energy to roll out of bed, and go through the motions of getting ready for school.

Mrs Shaw noticed the difference. "What's up this morning, Helen? You don't look very cheery."

"I don't feel very cheery," she replied gloomily.

"Why's that?"

"Don't know."

It was obvious that Helen wasn't in much of a mood for conversation, so her mother busied herself with making toast, chatting away while Helen listened.

A chill wind was blowing and a light drizzle falling by the time Helen was ready to leave for school. "You'll need your coat today," said her Mum, pulling it from a peg in the hallway and handing it to Helen. "I hope you feel better by this evening."

"Thanks. I'll see you later." Off Helen set, hunched behind the collar of her coat.

Wendy was waiting at the usual corner, glad to be able to shelter under a large tree. She greeted Helen with, "miserable day, isn't it?"

"It certainly is." Helen agreed so positively that Wendy reckoned she couldn't only be sharing her opinion about the weather.

"What's up then?"

"Nothing."

"Nothing? I don't believe that." Helen's mother might think it tactful not to persist in quizzing her daughter, but Wendy didn't believe in that kind of tact. "Come on, tell me what's bothering you."

"Nothing different."

"You mean, you're feeling depressed about Sam. Is that it?"

"Yes."

"Is he still in the cat and dog home?"

"Yes."

"And no-one has claimed him yet?"

"No."

"Hmm," Wendy sighed. The pair walked slowly in the direction of school. "So, are you no nearer your £50?"

"A bit," Helen replied.

"A bit? What does that mean? Have you got some money, then?"

Reluctantly Helen told her about the letter from Miss

Williams, and the £10 note tucked in with it. "That's marvellous," Wendy said. "You should be feeling great."

"I was last night. It seemed that at last I was getting somewhere. But..." Helen's voice trailed off.

"But...? But what?"

"But I can't see how I will ever have the other £40, and especially not by Monday morning at the latest." Her words were almost angry, and filled with despair.

"I see," Wendy mused. "On the other hand, you didn't have any idea how even £10 could come, and yet it did. So, if that can happen, why shouldn't the rest appear as well even if you don't know how?" There were moments, rare enough, when Wendy talked real sense, and that was one of them. Even Helen saw the point of her words, and brightened a little.

"Well, we'll see. Who knows how it could happen?"

"God does," said Wendy, even becoming spiritual for once. "I tell you, if God can produce £50 for you by Monday, you'll have even me believing in him! That would be something."

It certainly would, thought Helen, as they turned the corner and entered the school gates.

"Assembly day today - it's Friday," said Wendy. Their school had a full assembly only once a week, and this was the day.

The school bell sounded. The girls went briefly to their registration classes to be marked off for attendance, and five minutes later they were heading for the school hall. It only just held the 500 pupils plus staff.

The place buzzed with conversation. It was as if no-one ever listened, because all 500 voices seemed to speak simultaneously. Yet every pair of ears was attuned for the noise of the door at the rear of the hall. When it opened with a familiar creak, there was instantaneous silence. The headmaster entered, and walked towards the front. Dr Dunlop was not tall, but he was a formidable character. In the hush, his every footstep sounded loudly.

He climbed the half dozen steps on to the platform, looking serious as only headmasters can, and moved to the table in the middle. "Good morning school," his voice boomed.

"Good morning sir," chorused back 500 voices in a kind of unison.

"I'll not keep you too long this morning...," he continued.

'That's a pity,' thought Helen, because the longer assembly lasted the shorter was her first lesson, and it was maths. It was her least favourite subject, especially first thing in the morning. A reprieve from even five minutes of that was more than welcome.

"I have a few announcements for you," said Dr Dunlop. "First, I must remind you about next Wednesday when your parents are invited to meet your teachers and discuss your progress. It is particularly important that all of you deliver the letter with the details of this to your parents." Helen knew that more than a few in her class hadn't bothered, especially those with a reason why they didn't want their parents to hear about their progress.

"Then there's the frequent problem of litter in the

playground. I really do expect better standards from my pupils..." On droned the headmaster's voice. Helen's mood had sunk again, and mentally she switched off as the announcements, warnings, and encouragements continued from the platform. Her thoughts moved to her puppy with only one weekend left to live. She pictured Sam lying in a small basket, curled up tight against the cold wind of that grey morning. Was he as miserable as she was? Wasn't it unfair, she thought, that there was a little dog needing someone to care for him, and there was she, with all the care in the world for a little dog, and yet she couldn't have him? She couldn't see any sense in that, yet she couldn't change it.

"And finally..." The headmaster's voice broke back through her thoughts. He was finishing. Sometimes the headmaster fooled them by slipping in two 'And finally's'. "I have a special announcement for the First Year." Helen nudged Wendy, and Wendy nudged Helen. There was special interest in something concerning their year. Neither of them could risk getting into trouble for speaking, but they were each making sure the other was listening.

"Two weeks ago," continued the headmaster, "the English department set the First Year the task of writing an essay. Different classes were given different titles. One had to write on 'My home', another on 'My ambition', another on 'My family', and another on 'My pet'. What none of them knew was that these were not ordinary class essays, but were being assessed for a new and special award donated recently to the school. All the best essays were scrutinised by a small committee and I am now pleased to be able to announce the winner. It is..." His voice hesitated, and 100 First Year hearts pounded, "Helen Shaw, for an essay about her dog. Congratulations Helen, please come forward."

Helen nearly fainted as her name was announced. The hall burst into thunderous applause, and every eye turned in her direction. Her mind was in a spin, and she was hardly aware of Wendy pushing her along the row of seats, and out into the aisle. Somehow she found herself climbing the small flight of stairs on to the platform. The headmaster shook her hand warmly. As the applause subsided, he said, "I have a trophy here for you, Helen. It is of an old-fashioned quill pen, the sign of a writer. You'll find your name already inscribed near the bottom, and I hope you keep writing such good essays for many more years."

Helen somehow remembered to say "Thank you." The school applauded again, and she turned to leave the platform.

"Oh, one more thing I nearly forgot," said the headmaster, his voice barely audible above the sound of clapping. "There is another small reward which goes with the trophy." He handed Helen a white envelope.

She clutched it in one hand, the trophy in the other, and made her way carefully down the steps to ground level, and back to her seat. As she moved along her row, several fellow pupils patted her on the back.

"Well done, you clever so-and-so," Wendy dared to whisper as Helen regained her seat.

A moment later and assembly was dismissed. Out they trooped, Helen's thoughts still whirling like leaves in the wind. "I didn't know there was to be a prize," she said breathlessly.

"None of us did," said Wendy, "and if we had some of us might have tried a little harder." Her words sounded a little forlorn. "But you deserved it. You put your heart into that essay."

Helen rephrased Wendy's words. "I put what was on my heart into it."

"What's in the envelope?" Wendy asked.

Helen had forgotten about it, even though it was grasped firmly in her hand. "Oh, I've no idea."

"Well, open it and find out!" said Wendy with a grin.

Helen did as she was told, and found herself looking at a £20 note!

"£20?" said an amazed Wendy.

"£20" said an equally amazed Helen.

"Do you remember what I said to you on the way to school this morning?" Wendy asked, still hardly able to believe what she was seeing.

"I remember. I most certainly remember," answered Helen slowly.

Neither could speak another word, not even Wendy.

* * * *

Helen's mother and father were almost as excited as she was about the essay prize. Their meal was over, but they still sat at the table talking.

"Now where shall we put the trophy?" Mrs Shaw said.

"Nowhere too obvious, please," begged Helen.

"I'll be embarrassed if visitors notice it."

"Nonsense, I want them to notice it. I'd like them to know just how clever you are."

Helen groaned, but there was no way of dissuading her mother. The trophy was put on top of the piano. "It looks just fine there," Mrs Shaw announced, looking satisfied.

"You must be very pleased with yourself," said Helen's father. "It's quite something to be the best essay writer in the whole of First Year."

"I'm not complaining, especially since £20 came with the trophy."

Her Dad smiled. "I thought you might be at least as pleased with that as something which can be put on top of a piano. So, you're more than half way with the money?"

Helen gave a nervous shiver. "I know. And part of me is excited about how the rest is going to come in time, and another part of me is terrified in case it doesn't. There's only a couple of days left now."

"That's enough," said Mr Shaw. "If God means you to have this puppy, he's not going to give you the money too late."

"Okay, but how can he do it by Sunday?"

"Helen," her Mum joined in, "do you remember when you were very little, you asked lots of questions like, 'What's for tea?', 'Where are we going?' or 'What will it be like?', and we always gave you the same answer?" Helen smiled. She remembered those conversations very well. "And do you remember what that answer was?"

"Yes. You always told me to, 'Wait and see'."

"That's right. It wasn't always right or possible to tell you about something in advance. And when you did 'Wait and see', were you ever disappointed with the eventual outcome?"

"No, I don't think so."

"Well, sometimes God says 'Wait and see'. You're desperate to have this money, or at least to know how it'll come, but for his own good reasons God is saying 'Wait and see'. You won't be disappointed with what he does, I'm sure."

"You're becoming quite a theologian, Mum," teased Helen. "But you win," she conceded. "I'll wait and see what God does next."

Mr Shaw moved from the table, and made himself comfortable in his favourite arm chair. "Now," he said, "does your one and only father get to read your literary masterpiece, or does that honour go only to school teachers?"

"I might just grant you the privilege," said Helen as she headed for her bedroom to unearth the essay from its burial place in one of her folders. It took her longer than she'd anticipated to find it. 'It's remarkable how much junk accumulates in one week,' she said to herself. Her mind latched on to that thought. 'One week…is it really only one week since I came home with that essay?' Helen felt as if a lifetime had passed, so much had taken place in those seven days. Yet, with an unwelcome deadline for Sam's death looming, the week had also zoomed past. 'One week gone; one weekend left,' she thought.

Eventually she retrieved the essay, and brought it to her father. He settled even deeper into his chair, and began to read. Helen retreated to her bedroom. It clearly needed some tidying up, and being busy kept her mind from always thinking about Sam.

After a while, she heard a quiet knock at her door. "Come in," said Helen.

It was her father. "Can I have a word?"

"Of course," she replied, and moved a heap of books from the foot of her bed so he had somewhere to sit.

"It's about your essay," he began.

"Don't you like it? Do you not think it should have won the prize?"

Her father shook his head, but he was smiling. "Nothing like that could be further from my mind. Helen, what I came in here to say was that your essay about owning a dog deeply moved my heart. It was..." He hesitated, trying to find the right words. "It was so real. I could picture exactly how you felt about having a dog of your own, and the love and care which you'd give to it."

Helen found it difficult to look at her Dad. She stared down at the pattern on the carpet, but replied, "Thanks for saying you liked it."

"Well, let me add just this. I haven't got the money to allow you to go off and buy your little puppy in time. But if that money does come - and I'm praying for that to happen as well as you - then at least I know now that this is no idle whim to own a pet, and that you'll be a good and careful owner."

With that, he stood up, ready to leave. Helen's heart

suddenly felt ready to burst. His words had touched some of the deepest longings she had. Then the dam burst, and floods of tears flowed down her cheeks, while her body heaved and sighed with giant sobs. In an instant she flung herself into her father's arms, and he held on to her, patting her head gently, saying, "It's alright, Helen. It's all going to be alright." It was like when she was a little girl, and had fallen and hurt her knee or her arm, and came looking for comfort. Dad's hugs then had seemed to make all the difference. This time it was her heart which was hurting, and it felt good that he was still there to help her.

Chapter 8

Helen had worked it out. Realistically there were only two chances for the remaining £20 to come in enough time to save Sam. One was through the post on Saturday, and the other was a gift from someone at church on Sunday.

So she was downstairs by 8.30 a.m. that next morning, early for Helen on a Saturday. She peered out of the window and down the lane for the postman. "What time does he come usually?" she asked her mother.

"It can vary, depending on how many other letters he has to deliver. But I suppose he'll be here by around 9.30."

"Not until then?" Helen said, more than a little impatiently. But she busied herself organising her breakfast, and sat down at the kitchen table to eat it. Her Mum put a mug of tea in front of her.

"Don't get too worked up about this money, Helen. There's no reason why the postman should bring anything, is there?"

"No, but the money has to reach me somehow."

"That's true if you are meant to have this puppy. Perhaps you're not meant to have him, and then the money won't come."

"I am meant to have him, so the money must come," Helen said forcefully.

Mrs Shaw decided silence on that subject was wiser for the moment. Instead she asked, "What are you going to do today?"

"If the money comes, I'm going into town to get Sam from the cat and dog home. What else would I do?"

Her mother pursed her lips, and drew in her breath. Escaping from the subject of dogs wasn't easy. "Just suppose that the money doesn't come, which is possible, then what will you do?"

"I haven't thought about that."

"Try."

Helen tried, and eventually replied, "I guess I could give Wendy a call, and see if she has any plans. Perhaps some fresh air would help."

"That sounds fine. Mind you," her Mum continued, glancing out of the window as she spoke, "the weather doesn't seem any better today than yesterday. There are rather many dark clouds out there."

Just as she finished speaking, there was a clattering noise from the front door, followed by a gentle thump as something landed on the ground.

"It's the mail! The postman's early!" Helen shouted, and rushed through the house to see what had arrived. Her mother waited, breathing a silent prayer to God for either good news, or wisdom what to say if there was no news.

Helen was slow to return to the kitchen, and when she did Mrs Shaw didn't need a second glance at her downcast face to know there was nothing among the mail to encourage her daughter. "No money?" she asked gently.

"None," replied Helen. Her face was taut. She was trying to keep her emotions under control, and only just succeeding. "There's only two letters. One looks like another bill, and the other offers us free entry in a competition to win £50,000, but we would have to buy a £15 book from the company first."

Mrs Shaw took the letters from Helen. A quick look was all that was needed for her to decide to throw away the competition. The book they would have to buy was on how to organise family finances, and the last thing their finances needed was £15 spent on a book. She hesitated for a second before opening the other envelope, but there was nothing to be gained by delay. If it was a bill, it was a bill.

Helen watched her mother examine the contents. "More money wanted by someone?" she asked.

"Yes and no," came the reply. "It's from the telephone company. Not a bill, thankfully, but they are notifying us that the line rental and call charges will be increasing next month. So we will have to pay more eventually. Maybe we should give up having a phone…"

"Don't do that," Helen said quickly. "How would I be able to stay in touch with all my friends?"

"Perhaps you'd have to do it the old fashioned way, and walk to their homes. It might do you good." Helen shuddered at the thought. She didn't mind exercise, but she did appreciate the convenience of using the phone. Seeing her daughter's horror, her Mum added, "Perhaps it won't come to that. Wait and see."

"There's that phrase again," Helen said. "You told me to 'wait and see' what God would do about giving me the other £20, but he hasn't done it yet. There isn't much time left."

"But there is *enough* time," said her mother emphatically. "Besides, we haven't much choice, have we?"

"I don't suppose so," Helen admitted reluctantly.

They heard rain splattering against the window pane, and the wind begin to whistle through the trees. Both of them shivered.

"Looks like a day for going back to bed," Helen said gloomily.

"Don't be silly, you can't do that."

"There isn't much else worth doing." Helen rose from the table, and headed in the direction of her bedroom. When she got there, she picked up a book which she'd begun and found interesting. But she couldn't get back into the story, and tossed it aside after a couple of minutes.

She lay back on her bed, and stared hard at the ceiling. 'What a rotten, rotten day,' she thought.

Downstairs Mrs Shaw sat a moment longer at the kitchen table. Helen's feelings were soaring one minute and plunging the next, according to whether or not there was hope of saving 'her' puppy. She began to wish that the people who had dumped the puppy had picked some other lane, but then her conscience scolded her because that would have meant a little dog dying from lack of air tied up in a polythene bag.

"Well God," she prayed, "you allowed these people to put that dog in our lane just at the time Helen was passing. It looks like you meant her to find it, but if you did we need another £20 this weekend. I don't know any more than Helen does how that can happen. But, somehow, please make it happen."

And there Helen's mother sat for a long time, head buried in her hands. The sadness, uncertainty, and the urgency of it all was getting to her too.

* * * *

Helen woke up with a start. A loud crash had jolted her into consciousness. She hadn't meant to sleep, and she had no idea what time it was. She leant over from her bed, and lifted her small alarm clock. It was 1.00 p.m. She must have been asleep for three hours.

As Helen became more aware of her surroundings, she heard rain pounding against the window. The wind howled eerily round the chimney pots. Wearily Helen pulled herself off her bed. Her bones were stiff and sore. What made that loud noise which woke me up? she asked herself. One glance from her bedroom window answered her question. A huge branch from the tree in their back garden was lying on the ground. It must have been twelve or fourteen feet long, with lots of smaller branches making it six or seven feet wide. The weight of the branch had ploughed a deep furrow in the ground. 'That's not going to help Dad's vegetables to grow,' Helen thought mischievously. The tree trunk now had a jagged wound where the branch had been torn away by the wind.

From the window, Helen saw her father go outside to examine the branch. He had his large coat draped over his head in an attempt to keep dry, but the wind whipped it up continually. There was clearly nothing her father could do immediately about the fallen branch, and after the briefest of examinations he retreated back indoors.

Helen went downstairs to find both her parents staring out of the kitchen window at the garden. "You're alive, then," her Mum said.

"Seems so," Helen replied. "The weather hasn't improved, has it?"

"No, and the forecast says it'll get worse," said her Dad. "That branch coming down is bad enough. I just hope the tree is secure, because if it falls in any direction it'll fall on our house."

That startled Helen. Sure enough, that tree had always tilted towards their house. Once before, when she was about seven, she'd seen a house almost destroyed after a large tree had been blown on it in a storm. The roof had been smashed in, and the front wall had collapsed. "It won't really get blown over, will it?" she asked.

Her father grimaced, shaking his head slowly as he spoke. "I'm really not sure. I think it'll be okay providing the wind doesn't worsen. That branch coming down helps because it's one less to be caught by the gale."

"Is there anything we can do?" asked her mother.

"Not really," Mr Shaw replied. "There's no way to prop up a tree quickly. Anyway, it's alright at the moment, but just as a precaution let's stay away from this side of the house unless we must come here. Even then, let's keep it brief. If things get really serious, we may need to move out of our home until this storm subsides."

All three of them retreated through to their living room, which was towards the front of the house. Even though her father had said there was no immediate danger, Helen couldn't help feeling nervous. Her mind pictured that house she'd seen before, and it was hard not to imagine that at any moment their home would be smashed in two.

Half an hour later and Helen had a problem. "Dad," she said, "I need to go to the bathroom." That essential room was right under the overhanging tree.

Even though he was clearly worried, her father managed a smile. "It's alright, just go. We'll all have to before this storm is over. But don't take too long!"

Helen had never made a shorter visit to the bathroom. If her house was going to be destroyed, that was not the room she wanted rescuers to find her in. As fast as she could she returned to the safety of the living room.

She was lost for any good ideas of what to do. She tried reading, but none of her books really interested her at that moment. She thought TV might be the answer, but most channels were showing ancient films or sport on a Saturday afternoon. Sometimes Helen enjoyed the sports on TV, but no amount of switching programmes could get her away from either horse racing or ice hockey, both of which scored highly on her scales of boredom.

"Can I phone Wendy?" she asked her mother.

"Yes, that's fine."

Helen took the phone through to the hall, and dialled Wendy's number. "Hi - it's Helen," she said when her friend answered. "What's the weather like with you?"

"It sounds really stormy. My Dad went out to buy a newspaper, and said it was hard to keep his feet. Considering how overweight he is, that must be a powerful wind out there!" Wendy was often rude about her father's weight.

Helen added her own news about the broken branch, and how they were mostly staying on the safer side of the house.

"That sounds pretty scary," said Wendy.

"Only when you have to go to the bathroom," Helen laughed. "I'm not sure if we're going to eat much either, because the kitchen is also right under that tree."

"Why don't you all go out to a restaurant for a meal?"

"C'mon, Wendy. You know better than that. There's no way my Dad can afford to take us all out at the moment. Probably what'll happen is that Mum will make a dash for the bread and a few other things, and we'll have a sandwich picnic in our living room. We'll survive."

The phone line became crackly. "It's probably interference because of the storm," said Wendy. "Listen, before you go, tell me if there have been any new developments about the puppy."

"There's nothing new, nothing at all."

"So what's going to happen?"

"If I get the money by tomorrow, I can save Sam. If not…" Helen paused, then added, "I guess he dies."

"Surely not, Helen? There must be something you can do."

"Wanting to do something, and actually being able to do it are very different. I can tell the cat and dog home how much I want a puppy, but if I don't have the money, they can't keep feeding and housing him until I get it."

"But what about your parents? Won't they change their minds?"

"I don't think so, partly because there really is no money to spend on a dog, and partly because they believe it will only be right to have Sam if the money comes in time. They see the money appearing as a kind of test to show whether or not it's right to have a dog."

"Can't you argue them out of that?"

"I don't think so, and - if I'm really honest - I don't think I should. If they had pots of money, it might be fair to try and make them think differently. But already Dad doesn't know where the money will come from to pay a number of bills, so I can hardly put them under even more pressure. I suppose I should be grateful they'll even think about having Sam."

Wendy blew gently through her cheeks. "I'm not sure I could see it that way."

"I haven't got any option," said Helen.

They chatted some more. Helen asked if Wendy wanted to meet up with her later, but both eventually agreed that the weather was so bad it would be an evening to stay in and keep warm. By now it was becoming increasingly difficult to make out what each other was saying because of noise on the phone line. They said their farewells, and hung up.

"Is Wendy fine?" asked her mother as Helen came back into the room.

"Yes, she's okay. I don't think she's very much to do either, but it's not a day for getting out and about."

"It certainly isn't," agreed Mrs Shaw.

Helen picked up a magazine, and stretched out on the long sofa, trying to read. She almost managed to get interested in the letters on the 'Problems Page', and wondered what advice the columnist would give to an eleven-year-old girl who wanted a dog of her own.

Suddenly an almighty crash destroyed her daydreaming. Helen jumped up from the sofa. "The tree's coming down!" she shouted.

"No it's not, but something has fallen," said Mr Shaw, who was even quicker off the mark than Helen in heading towards the rear of the house. Mrs Shaw was last in line. She had been dozing peacefully in her armchair until rudely awakened by the crash and Helen's shout. "I'm more at risk of dying from fright by you shouting than from any tree," she mumbled at Helen.

A moment later all three of them stood at the side of the house, looking at smashed fragments of a chimney pot strewn over the ground.

"Well, if that's the worst of it, it's not too bad," said Mr Shaw.

"Another bill, though?" asked Helen.

"I think this one will be covered by our insurance

policy - thankfully," her father replied.

"I'm glad no-one was in the garden at the moment that came down," said Mrs Shaw.

"You're right," agreed Mr Shaw. "Let's just stay indoors, and say our prayers. This storm can't last forever."

Chapter 9

Late that night the storm was continuing to roar outside. Rain pelted down, forming large puddles on the lane. Mr Shaw had gone out briefly to look around the house in case there was any more damage. He'd come back breathless with the effort of resisting the powerful wind and driving rain. He had decided the house was safe enough, but told Helen she should sleep downstairs in the living room rather than her own room which was too near the leaning tree.

The mattress from Helen's bed had been dragged downstairs, and she was comfortable enough on that, wrapped round with the sleeping bag normally used on camping holidays. Although she didn't feel entirely safe, there was enough of the little girl left inside Helen to regard all this drama as a bit of an adventure.

As she lay on the floor, she could hear occasional sounds from the distance of splintering wood as branches crashed to the ground. Both the television and radio news bulletins had highlighted what they called 'freak weather' sweeping across the country. There had been dramatic pictures of flooded rivers, and of trees which had demolished parked cars and blocked roads. Thankfully there seemed to have been no serious injuries, but there were warnings from the police that no-one should make any unnecessary journeys. The weather forecasters said there was no sign yet of the storm dying down.

Sleep would not come for Helen. In the darkness, the biggest storm of all seemed to be raging inside her heart. Thoughts darted through her mind faster than the wind blowing outside. Why had she found Sam a week ago if he was still to die? Was there any hope now for the £20 she still needed? Had God really meant her to believe that she was to have this puppy? Had she turned her own wishful thinking into the will of God?

She knew what she believed, but did she only believe it because she wanted to believe it? Could her hopes ever come to anything? Questions, questions, plenty of questions.

'If only there was more time…' Helen thought. 'And yet, what difference would that make? Well, at least that would give a greater chance of finding the money I need to buy Sam. But if the money doesn't come this weekend, would it be right for me to buy him at all?' On and on went the argument inside her mind.

Helen tossed and turned from one side to the other. She felt so tired, and yet she couldn't sleep. Her mind danced, and her emotions felt like a punchbag being pounded by a championship boxer.

She picked up her clock and glanced at its illuminated face. It was one o'clock in the morning. Helen groaned. She knew how tired she'd feel in a few hours time when she was due to get up. 'I've got to sleep,' she told herself. But she couldn't.

She lay flat on her back, and stared straight up. There was nothing to see. Because she lived outside the town, there were no street lights to shine into the room. Sometimes the moon was bright enough to allow her to glimpse a little, but the clouds scudding across the sky made an effective blackout this night.

Helen felt desperate. She couldn't continue like this until Monday. She wasn't sure she could even cope with her inner panic until morning. Something had to change.

Helen gritted her teeth. It was time for another determined prayer. "God," Helen said, "you know exactly how I'm feeling, and you know my doubts as well as my faith. Please let me know what's right about Sam. Please show me whether I should still hope or give up on the idea of having my own puppy. I need help - somehow! And don't be angry if I say I need it now..."

It was good to get those words out. Now she waited. She wondered if she'd be given the same kind of certainty as a week before. Would she hear a voice speak from heaven? Would there be a glow in the dark to indicate God's presence? Would an angel come and talk with her? Something had to happen.

Something did.

Helen heard a gentle tap at the door. She wanted to panic, but she managed to stammer, "Yes Lord...I'm here."

Through the wind, she heard a voice, and it called quietly, "Helen, Helen..."

"Yes, yes," she called back.

The door began to open. Helen thought she was

going to die. More than anything she wanted an answer to her prayer, but she had never imagined it would come this direct. In terror she buried her head inside her sleeping bag, and lay there waiting.

A moment later and she felt a hand rest on her. "Helen, are you awake?" asked a voice.

'I'm awake, but I'm not coming out...' Helen thought to herself. But even as she thought it, she realised that the voice she heard so indistinctly because of the storm and her sleeping bag was a little familiar. Another moment's thought, and she knew it was very familiar.

She popped her head out of her cocoon. "Mum?" she said.

"Yes," her mother replied. "Who did you think it would be?"

"Oh Mum. You nearly gave me heart failure."

"I'm sorry, my dear. I couldn't sleep because of the storm, and I thought you might still be awake too and a bit frightened down here on your own, so I came to see if you wanted a cup of tea. How about it?"

"I didn't need it before, but I certainly need it now," Helen gasped.

* * * *

For once Helen was probably more glad of a cup of tea than her mother. She sat up on her mattress, still half covered by her sleeping bag. Slowly the tension and fright eased away.

"I can't remember when we last had a storm this bad," her mother said. "I suspect we're getting it a bit worse than some of the homes in town because we don't have other houses around us like they do to give some shelter."

"I keep hearing noises in the distance," Helen chipped in. "I think quite a number of branches are falling. It's good to be indoors."

They had put on a small table light, and the warm glow helped them feel safe. Anything was preferable to total darkness.

"There are always some people who have to go out on nights like this," her mother remarked. "There's policemen, and ambulancemen and firemen when there are accidents."

"What do the firemen do?"

"Often they're the only ones with equipment to cut people free if they're trapped in their homes or cars by falling trees."

"That must be difficult in the middle of the night."

Her Mum nodded in agreement. "Are you feeling better now?"

"A bit - the cup of tea helps."

"It always does. I don't know how I'd manage if tea hadn't been discovered."

Helen laughed. "I think you'd have invented something like it yourself if it hadn't existed." Then she became serious. "Mum, how can I know for sure if God really told me Sam would be mine?"

Mrs Shaw frowned, not out of anger but an inability to answer her daughter's questions in a way that would satisfy her. "I'm not much good at theology in the middle of the night, Helen."

"It's a simple question Mum."

"The question's fine. It's the answer I'm having problems with. Let me think."

"All I really want to know is whether you believe it's still possible that God will do something to save Sam."

"It's possible," Mrs Shaw said hesitantly.

"I don't want you to say that in the ordinary sense of possible. I mean, do you think he'll do it?"

"That's harder, isn't it? Helen, I can't know for sure one way or the other what God will do. Let me say this, though. There isn't much time left, and I've no idea how you can have another £20 by tomorrow night, but God is a God of the impossible and he has so often surprised me in the past I'm prepared to be surprised again."

"If you were me, would you still have hope?"

Mrs Shaw moved from her chair to sit on the mattress alongside her daughter. Her words sounded soft yet serious against the background of wind and rain. "Helen, let me tell you something you've never heard before."

Helen pulled the sleeping bag around her shoulders to keep herself warm, and listened carefully to her mother.

"When I was around twenty-one, your Dad and I got to know each other. We were boyfriend and girlfriend. And that was very special. From the earliest days of our friendship, I knew that your Dad was the right one for me. The more I prayed about it, the more I believed that God meant us to be together forever. But we split up."

"Why?"

Her mother took a deep breath. "Because your Dad

met someone else."

"Another woman?!" Helen asked with a mixture of intrigue and pretend horror.

Mrs Shaw smiled. "That's right. He began to go out with someone else. Perhaps you can imagine how I felt."

"Pretty upset, I guess."

"That's putting it mildly. And it got worse and worse. I still saw your Dad from time to time, and from what he said and friends told me, I could see this other relationship was getting more and more serious. Everyone expected them to get engaged."

Helen sat quietly, waiting while her mother sipped her tea. "I prayed, asking God if what I had believed about your Dad and me was wrong. I thought that maybe I'd just come to love him, and then turned that love into the will of God to make it seem right. But nothing changed. I still loved him, and I still believed God wanted us together."

"What happened?" Helen asked.

"His romance with this other young woman headed towards its first anniversary. It seemed sure that would become the date on which they would announce their engagement."

"Did they?"

"No, they didn't. In fact, the opposite happened. Right on one year of being together they decided to end the relationship."

"You must have been relieved."

"That probably ranks as the understatement of the century."

"So, did he come back to you after that?"

"I wouldn't phrase it like that, but yes, he did. Your Dad had learned some hard lessons during that year, including what it was to really love someone and what it meant to be committed. Within a few months we were engaged. Within a year we were married."

"That quick?"

"Yes - but when the time comes don't you be in as much of a hurry! Unless, I suppose, you meet someone as wonderful as your Dad, and you're as sure as I was." They both smiled. "Helen, I've not been telling you all this just to amuse you in the night. What I'm saying is that at one time I was really sure something was right even though all the signs were against it coming true. During that year when your Dad was seeing someone else, lots of people told me to forget him, that I was wasting my time in hoping we would ever get together again. But I knew he was the right one for me, and I believed God wanted us for each other. I couldn't give him up. I couldn't believe something different from what I believed. I think you understand that."

Helen nodded her head vigorously. "That's right. I can't give up what I know is right."

"And I don't blame you." Mrs Shaw stood up to go. "The ultimate proof of my convictions was when your Dad and I were married. In your case the proof will be if the money is there in time to save Sam. If you're right, we'll rejoice with you. If you're wrong, we'll cry with you."

"Thanks Mum, you've really helped me." Helen burrowed deep down into her sleeping bag, laying her head back on the pillow.

Mrs Shaw bent over and kissed Helen lightly on the forehead. "Sleep well, my special Helen." Then she switched off the light, and in a moment was gone.

Helen felt better inside than she'd done for days. Within two minutes she was asleep. The only thought she had before her eyes closed was to wonder if, instead of angels, God sometimes sent mothers to answer prayers.

Chapter 10

By morning the rain had eased a little, but not the storm force wind. Helen gazed out the living room window watching clouds racing by, distant trees bucking in the wind as if being tortured.

"We've lost a few more small branches, but at least the tree is still standing," said Mr Shaw as he brought in his breakfast. "I listened to the weather report on the radio earlier, and the forecaster said there had been 100 mile per hour gusts in exposed places overnight."

Mrs Shaw was pushing Helen's mattress to one side to give herself room to sit down. "Did he say the storm would pass soon?" she asked.

"I'm afraid he said it would probably last through most of today, which is not good news."

Helen turned away from the window. She picked up a bowl of cereal her mother had brought through for her. "It looks as though there'll be quite a number of branches across the lane," she said between mouthfuls. "We'll maybe have to clear a path to get to church."

Her Dad shook his head. "I don't think we'll be able to go this morning. The weather is really too fierce to venture out, and I don't want to leave this house when there's still some danger of the tree at the back being blown down. Someone would have to be around to deal with the damage if that happened."

Helen couldn't believe her father's words. "We've got to go to church. It's absolutely vital."

Mr Shaw raised his eyebrows in surprise. "This is a little more enthusiasm than normal, Helen."

"Well," she said, feeling a little flustered. "We always go to church, and we shouldn't be stopped by a little bit of wind blowing."

"It's not a little wind..." Mr Shaw began to say, but Mrs Shaw intervened to keep the peace.

"I don't think Helen's concern about church has much to do with the severity or otherwise of the wind. It may be more about whether there's someone at church who will feel led to give her a gift of some money."

"I see," nodded Mr Shaw. "You believe someone might have that £20 you need to buy Sam."

"Well...yes. I can't imagine any other way I'm going to get it at this late stage. So I must go. It's Sam's last chance."

"Emm...I'll think about it. You go off and get dressed while your mother and I have a chance to talk."

Helen zoomed out of the room at top speed, and got herself ready as if going to church. She was sure her Mum could put over her case convincingly. She had a way of getting her husband to agree. Helen was back in the room within ten minutes.

"That was quick!" her mother said smiling. "You can certainly move fast when you want to."

"Here's what's going to happen," said Mr Shaw.

"You and your mother can go to church, but I'm going to stay here to keep an eye on the property. Is that alright with you?"

Helen's face lit up. "Fine! No complaints from this department."

"And Helen," he added. "Remember what church is really for, and try not to look as though you're only there hoping for money."

"I'll try," she replied with a grin. Then looking around at her mother, she said, "C'mon Mum. I'm ready to go, and you're not even dressed yet. I can't imagine what's been keeping you."

"Cheeky young lady," Mrs Shaw murmured, but not at all angrily. She glanced at her watch. "I may not be able to get myself organized quite as quickly as you, but since it's still two hours until we need to leave, I reckon there's a chance I can have my Sunday best clothes on by then."

* * * *

The drive into town was far from easy. This was the first time either Helen or her mother had been out properly in the storm, and neither of them had guessed just how vicious the gusts of wind could be. Mrs Shaw found she had to grip the steering wheel of the car with extra firmness, and to keep the speed down, because the wind could easily have blown the car far enough sideways to force them into a ditch or to collide with a wall. If that wasn't difficult enough, the rain blown against the windscreen made it hard to see where to go.

Helen had a rougher time still. As she'd predicted,

there were many branches strewn over their lane and even on the main road. Every now and then Mrs Shaw had to brake, and Helen dashed out to pull a branch out of the way. She wondered why she'd ever bothered to brush her hair that morning. Five seconds in the wind had turned her into a good imitation for a scarecrow.

"There are not many other cars about," Helen said as she climbed back into the car after heaving yet another branch to the side of the road.

"Well, there's never much traffic on a Sunday morning, and especially not today. I don't think many will come out if they have any choice."

They finally managed to negotiate their way into town, and parked the car nearer to church than was usually possible. "There certainly can't be a big turnout at the service this morning," Mrs Shaw said.

"As long as the right people are here," Helen said, determined to believe someone would have a gift for her.

Hurriedly they clambered up the front steps of the church building, and found their usual seats. Helen glanced around nervously, checking out those who had made it. Her mother had been right, however. Probably no more than half the usual number were there. Helen grimaced, but bent her head and said a quiet prayer.

The congregation waited patiently for the service to begin. The normal starting time was 11.00 a.m., and when five minutes past eleven came and went, there was a stir among the people. Another five minutes elapsed. Helen saw the elderly man seated in front of her take off his watch and give it a shake, oblivious to the fact that there was nothing to shake in a digital watch.

Yet more time passed. At 11.20 a.m. a door near the front opened, and one of the church's elders came on to the platform. "I'm sorry you have had to wait. Our minister has just succeeded in telephoning through to our church office. As you know, once a month he takes an early service in an outlying village. He managed to reach there with great difficulty this morning, and then set off to drive back here. Apparently, as he rounded a sharp corner he found the huge branch of a tree lying in the road, and was unable to stop before crashing into it."

There was a murmur among the people, matched with many worried looks.

"I am happy to be able to report that our minister was unharmed, but unfortunately his car was damaged to the extent that he cannot drive it, and he will have to wait until a rescue vehicle comes to tow it away. That may take some time since all the rescue services are very busy today. Therefore, he wants me to convey his most profound apologies that he will not be able to be with us this morning." The elder paused to clear his throat, and then continued. "I believe that under these circumstances many would be happy to get back to their own homes sooner rather than later, so I propose we sing one hymn after which I will lead us in prayer, and then we will conclude our service."

The hymn was announced, the prayer offered, and the service ended.

"That must set a new record for short church services," Helen whispered to her mother.

"At least there won't be any complaints today that everything dragged on too long," she whispered back.

"I'm off to chat to a few people," Helen said.

"Alright, but be careful what you say Helen. You mustn't try and take God's work away from him." Helen nodded.

She walked quickly to the entrance vestibule of the church. That was a large area, and usually plenty people stood around there chatting as if they didn't have homes to go to.

But not that Sunday. Everyone seemed to gather their coats, and set off into the wind immediately. Other than the odd murmuring of "Hello, terrible storm isn't it?", no-one seemed to want to stop and talk to an eleven-year-old girl.

The sense of panic began to rise again inside Helen. This wasn't how it was meant to happen. Then she saw her friend, Miss Williams, coming her way. This could be it. Maybe she felt led to give even more money. "Good morning, Helen," she said. "How are you?"

"I'm fine, thanks. Thank you for your letter and the money you gave."

"I just felt that was right. Has the rest of the money come yet?"

"No, not yet."

Miss Williams turned up the collar of her coat, in readiness to brave the wind. "Well, keep praying," she said. "I'm sure it'll come in time."

With that she was gone. Helen felt dazed. She wanted to call after her that there was no more time. She needed the rest of the money now. Next week wouldn't do. But she'd gone.

Helen turned round again, looking back into the church. Almost the only one still there was her mother, watching with a love which hurt at seeing her daughter so sad. Mrs Shaw moved forward, and put her arm around Helen's shoulders. "I'm sorry Helen. Come on, let's go home." Out into biting wind and driving rain they went, where people would think their moist eyes were only smarting from the gale.

* * * *

Most of the journey home was made in silence. Helen had nothing to say. Her mother could think of nothing to say which would help. The driving was still difficult, so Mrs Shaw concentrated as hard as she could on that. Every now and again they came on more branches blocking their path either partially or completely, and Helen had to move them. At one point Mrs Shaw had to steer sideways to avoid a waste bin propelled down the street by the storm. Both wished they were already home. The journey seemed to last forever.

"What will you do this afternoon?" Mrs Shaw asked eventually.

"I don't know. I guess there's some reading I could do."

"That may be best. It isn't going to be an afternoon to go for a walk. This wind seems every bit as strong as it was last night."

They settled into an uneasy quiet again. There were only one or two more corners to be negotiated, and thankfully they turned out to be without incident. Mrs Shaw swung the car into their lane. Home was in sight.

Suddenly she stopped. "What's the matter?" Helen asked wearily.

"The house. Something's wrong."

Both of them stared ahead. The house was the same as ever, and yet it wasn't. It was like a well known jigsaw puzzle with some pieces missing or moved, but neither could quite see what was different.

The awful answer dawned on Helen first. "The tree!" she shouted, "the tree! It isn't there any more."

Normally the huge, leaning tree behind their house could be seen easily as it towered high above their roof. But not now.

"Oh no!" said Mrs Shaw, "it must have come down with the wind. What's happened to your Dad? We must see what's happened to your Dad. I hope he's alright."

She rammed the car into gear, and drove it insanely fast up the lane. Thankfully only small branches lay on the lane, and the car crunched over them without danger. "At least the tree has missed landing on the house," Mrs Shaw said hastily. "It seems to be lying to one side." They screeched to a halt at their front door.

Helen leapt out of the car, but her mother was even quicker. Together they raced through the front door. "George! George! Are you alright?" called Mrs Shaw. There was no answer.

"I'll check upstairs," Helen shouted, and sped up the stairs. Again there was no sign of her father. "I can't see him," she reported back. "Where is he? What's happened to him?" A terrible dread was beginning to seize Helen's heart.

"He might have gone outside," said her Mum, sounding calmer than she felt.

The door to the back garden was on the side of the house. It was unfastened. "You're right, he has gone out," Helen said, pulling it open.

But that was as far as they could go because they were met with a wall of branches, twigs and leaves. The thick mass of the fallen tree blocked the way.

"George! George! Are you there?" Mrs Shaw shouted. Her only answer was the sound of the wind whipping through the leaves.

"I'll run round from the front and look," Helen called, already on her way. That was no easy task either, however, because the tree filled the whole space between their house and the wall at the edge of the garden. Thankfully, though, the branches near what had been the top of the tree weren't so thick, and Helen was able to push many of them aside and clamber inside the tree.

Twigs tore at her skirt, guaranteeing it would never be worn again to church. Helen didn't care. She pushed deeper into the dense foliage. Her hair snagged on a branch, and she felt a sharp stab of pain. "Ouch!" she cried, and had to move backwards to free herself. A moment later she pressed forward again.

Her search seemed hopeless, though, because the density of crushed wood and leaves meant she couldn't see more than six inches in front of her at a time. "I can't get through all this!" she shouted in despair.

"Keep trying Helen," her mother called back,

"because I can't find your Dad anywhere else."

With all the energy she possessed Helen pulled at the branches in front of her, squeezing through tiny gaps.

Suddenly her heart leapt into her mouth. Down near the ground she could see a hand. "Dad! DAD!" There was no reply. "Mum! He's here, buried by the tree." Helen tore frantically at leaves and branches, pushing herself forward, hardly noticing how much it hurt or what it did to her clothing. 'Oh God, please don't let Dad be dead, she prayed. I don't care if I never have a dog. Please let my Dad be alright...'

"Helen, what's happening. Can you get to him?" Her mother was desperate with worry, unable to see anything from her position at the side door.

"I'm almost there," Helen gasped back. "Hang on..." She broke the last branch in her way with a strength she never knew she had. "Right, I'm there!"

Her father's chest and legs were pinned to the ground by branches more than twelve inches thick. He lay ominously still, his face white except where blood had oozed from a deep gash on his forehead. Helen felt ill with fear.

"Mum, we're going to need help. Dad doesn't look in a good way at all, and we'll never be able to get the branches off him."

"Right, I'll phone the police for them to get someone with tree cutting equipment. And I'll send for an ambulance... You stay with your Dad."

Mrs Shaw's voice trailed off as she ran inside, but a moment later she was back. It was too quick for her to have made the calls. "Our phone isn't working. The tree will have pulled the telephone line down when it fell. We're cut off!"

"Okay. I'll get help," Helen shouted back. For a second she held her father's hand softly. Then she retreated out of the tree as fast as she could, shaking herself free from the snares of the branches, not caring how much the sharp digs hurt in her back and legs. A minute later she was clear.

Her Mum had come round to the front. "I'll run to the nearest house," Helen gasped, already breathless.

"Be as quick as you can Helen," said Mrs Shaw. But her words were unnecessary. Helen was already on her way.

Down the lane she sped as fast as her legs could be made to move. The shoes she had worn to church were never made for running, and slowed her down as they caught in the muddy ground. Helen paused long enough to pull them off, then ran on clutching her shoes in her hand. The loose stones on the lane pricked at her feet, but Helen hardly felt the pain. Just occasionally she winced when her toe struck a small boulder.

There were plenty of potholes, filled with muddy brown water from the torrential rain. Helen's clothes were soon splattered, and she felt the mud cover her hair and face as she splashed through the largest of the puddles. On and on she ran, though, thinking only of getting to the outskirts of town where someone would let her use a phone.

She felt her legs begin to weaken. Her breath came in short gasps. But Helen wouldn't let up. In her mind she saw her father's pale face, and that hand lying limp on the ground. "God, get me there somehow. I must get help for my Dad. I love him. I don't want him to die." She shouted her prayer out loud. There was no-one to hear but God.

A moment later and she was at the main road. She turned towards town and ran hard. She'd hardly gone more than fifty metres when she heard a car behind her. She paused, looking back. The car slowed as it came nearer, and to Helen's utter amazement she saw that it was a police car.

Helen stood panting for breath, as the car pulled up. There were two policemen inside, and one leaned out of his window to speak to Helen. "Is everything alright, young lady? You were running pretty fast." He glanced at the mud which seemed to cover her from head to foot. "And you look in a bit of a state."

"It's my Dad," Helen said, gasping for air, the words coming out jerkily. "The tree behind our house...it's fallen...Dad's trapped...he's unconscious...or dead."

"Jump in the back," the policeman said quickly. Helen obeyed. "Now show us where he is."

In a second the car had turned, and Helen guided them back up her lane. Her Mum had gone fast, but the police driver went even faster. They screeched to a halt, and instantly one of them was out of the car, heading for the tree at the side of the house. The other policeman stayed back to radio for help.

"Your Dad is under there?" the first policeman asked Helen.

"Yes. I think my Mum will have crawled in to be

beside him."

"Right, we'll see what we can do but we'll need major cutting gear to free him completely." The policeman nodded to his colleague, and he began to radio his base for help.

Mrs Shaw had heard voices, and disentangled herself from the tree slowly to find out what was happening. She was very relieved to see Helen, especially with two policemen.

"How is your husband?" asked the nearest policeman when she got clear of the tree.

"Not good, but I know he's still alive. I managed to trace a pulse in his wrist."

Helen felt a mountain of tension collapse inside her when she heard that her Dad was still alive. She'd really feared he wouldn't be. Tears flowed, and her body was racked by huge sobs which she couldn't control. Her Mum moved over to her, and pulled Helen into her arms. "It's alright, Helen. You've done all you can."

The second policeman appeared, carrying an axe and some rope which he'd brought from the rear of the car. "This won't be enough to get him out," he said, "but at least we can begin to clear the way so that the ambulancemen who are coming can get to him. Just stand clear."

The policemen set to work. Helen and her Mum watched, crying, praying, hoping.

Chapter 11

The policeman who had radioed for help had sent for powerful chain saws, but it appeared that the men operating them were busy elsewhere clearing fallen trees. "They're coming as soon as they can," he said, "but they've a bit of a journey to get here, so I'm afraid there will be a delay."

Mrs Shaw glanced at Helen, and saw fear written all over her exhausted face. "Let's be brave Helen. Dad's in God's hands, and there's nowhere safer."

She'd hardly finished speaking when an ambulance roared up the lane. "Good," said the policeman standing alongside them. "At least it's been able to come quickly."

The other policeman had been busy wielding the axe, and within a few more minutes had cleared a path through the more superficial branches to allow the ambulancemen to reach Mr Shaw. In they went, and began to monitor the trapped man's breathing and pulse.

After a while, one ambulanceman crawled back out. "How is he?" Mrs Shaw asked anxiously.

"It's too early to say, I'm afraid. The good news is that he's still alive. He could easily have been killed outright." He paused, as if wondering how much to tell Mrs Shaw. "It looks as though at least one of his legs is broken. That's bad but not serious. The real danger areas are across his chest and to his head. There's no way of knowing how much damage was done there until we get him to hospital." The ambulanceman gritted his teeth. "We must get him there soon, but we could never lift those huge branches."

Time had never seemed to pass so slowly. The wind was still blowing as furiously as ever, and the rain kept coming in occasional downpours, but no-one seemed to notice. All Helen could do was scan the distant road for any vehicle which looked as though it might be the van carrying men with chain saws. She looked at her watch. It was 1.30. It crossed her mind that they would normally be sitting down to Sunday lunch at that time. Today she had not the slightest interest in food.

Helen sat down on the stone step at the front of the house, burying her head in her hands. She had never felt despair and fear like this. Her father really could die. A moment later she sensed someone beside her, and an arm slipped round her shoulders. It was her Mum. "Are you okay?" she asked gently.

"Mum, all this is my fault. I'm so sorry." Tears came with the words.

"Your fault? Why is it your fault?" her mother asked.

"I'm the one who insisted on going to church. I shouldn't have done that on a day like this, but I thought someone there would give me money for Sam. I'm so selfish. If only we hadn't gone, then maybe Dad would have stayed in the front of the house with us and wouldn't have been hit by the tree."

"Helen, Helen, Helen..." said her mother, resting her daughter's head on her shoulder. "Every time something bad happens in life, we can look back and say, 'If only this had been different,' or 'if only I'd done that another way'. But that's hindsight. When you take decisions, you don't know the future. All you can do is what seems right at that time."

"But I didn't *know* it was right to go to church today. I wanted to be there for my own reasons."

"Well, God knew all that was going to happen. This accident didn't catch him by surprise. He'll look after Dad. You wait and see."

A little hope rose inside Helen. But it didn't last long. Another of the ambulancemen appeared from inside the tree, and he spoke anxiously to a policeman. "This man needs to get to hospital now. His pulse is weakening. Is there anything you can do to hurry things up?" Only as he finished did he realise Helen and her mother were able to hear. It was too late now though to spare them more worry.

"I'll do what I can," the policeman replied, "but they've a lot of miles to cover, and there could be many trees in their way." He moved over to his car, and got on the radio again.

Helen felt an overwhelming temptation to panic, but she resisted it. 'Alright God,' she prayed. 'Since you knew this would happen, please also give us a way out of it.' She stood up, and walked along the lane, looking anxiously for some sign of help arriving. But there was nothing. She turned back, surveying the police car and ambulance pulled up alongside their own car in front of the house. Of all the things she expected to happen this weekend, this was not one of them.

Her eyes drifted to the massive fallen tree lying alongside the house. At that moment a crazy idea filled her mind.

She ran quickly to the nearest policeman. "I think I know a way to get my father out from under the tree," she said.

The tall policeman looked down at her. "I know you mean to help, young lady. But this is a job for experts, and they'll come as soon as they can. There's no way we can lift the tree."

Helen wasn't going to be put off. "Just listen to me, please!" When she was worked up, Helen was a match for anyone.

"Alright, what's on your mind?" the policeman conceded.

Helen spoke fast. "You've got some rope, and so have we in our back shed. If you look at our house, our chimney stack is right above where the tree fell. Suppose we tie both ropes to the tree, and throw the other ends over the roof, inside the stack. Then we can pull on them to lift the tree just enough to get Dad out. It would be like having a pulley."

The policeman stared up, studying the chimney stack. "These things are not always secure," he murmured.

"Ours is," Helen insisted. "Look at it...our whole house is stone built, including the chimney stacks."

The policeman gazed again. "It might work…"

One of the ambulancemen had overheard the conversation. "Unless the fellows with the chain saws are going to be here very soon, it may be the only chance this fellow under the tree has got."

"Okay, let's have a go," the policeman said.

It didn't take them long to get organised. The ropes were quickly tied in place, the other ends flung high over the top of the house and pulled tight against the chimney stack. The two policemen took hold of one rope, and Mrs Shaw, Helen, and one of the ambulancemen stood ready with the other. The second ambulanceman was in position inside the tree, ready to pull Mr Shaw clear once the weight was off him. He was in the most dangerous position, because if either rope broke the tree could crash back and injure him as well.

"We don't have to lift this tree more than a few inches," one policeman instructed. "All we need to do is get it up, hold it for a few seconds until the casualty is pulled clear, then we can let go. But we'd better do that gently, or someone will have their hands burned by the rope. Does everyone understand?" They all nodded. "Are you ready at the tree?" he called to the ambulanceman.

"Ready!" came the reply.

"On the count of three," said the policeman, beginning to take the strain on the rope. "One - Two - THREE!"

Policemen, ambulanceman, and the two women pulled on their ropes with all the strength they possessed. The tree began to shake, but barely budged. "Come on,

HEAVE...!" called the policeman. Every muscle tightened in Helen's body. The rope hurt her hands, but she pulled harder and harder. Her face contorted with the strain. Slowly the tree inched upwards.

"Hold it there! Now just hold it!" called a voice from inside the tree. "I can get him..."

Keeping that tree up seemed almost harder than lifting it. Helen thought her arms were going to be pulled from their sockets. Her hands began to slip, but she gripped even tighter, ignoring the pain. She was determined that she would not let go...for her Dad's sake.

Seconds passed but it seemed like hours. Then the voice shouted, "It's okay! He's clear. You can let it down."

With immense relief, all five relaxed their pull on the ropes, and the tree fell back into place with a gentle crash.

The second ambulanceman ran to his vehicle and fetched a metal stretcher. He separated it into two halves lengthwise, and then joined his colleague among the lighter twigs at the edge of the tree. Anxiously Helen and her mother watched them slide each part in turn under Mr Shaw's body, join them again, and carry him clear of the tree.

"Right, let's get this man to hospital fast!" one of the policemen said. "We'll give you an escort." He turned towards Mrs Shaw. "You and your daughter can go in the ambulance as well if you want. But hang on!"

Everyone scrambled into their places, one ambulanceman at the wheel, and the other tending to Mr

Shaw now installed securely in the rear. Helen and her mother found seats, and gripped tightly. The blue lights on the roofs of the police car and the ambulance began to flash, and a second later they were off.

Helen had no idea any vehicle could go as fast as these did. In mere seconds they reached the main road, the ambulance was flung round the corner and zoomed into town. Whenever they came near to traffic or a road junction, the police car's siren was switched on, and they were able to get a clear way through.

"He's a tough man," the ambulanceman said who was monitoring Mr Shaw's condition. "He's doing well all things considered."

Mrs Shaw nodded, grateful for any encouragement. In less than ten minutes they were screeching into the Accident and Emergency bay of the hospital. The ambulance driver had radioed ahead to say they were coming, and hospital staff were ready to help carry Mr Shaw inside.

"Leave us to have a look at him, and we'll tell you how he is as soon as possible," a young doctor said hurriedly. Helen and her mother were suddenly alone by the entrance door. A kind nurse took one look at them, and said, "I think you could do with somewhere to wait which is a bit private. Would you like a cup of tea?" They nodded.

Helen slumped in a seat, while Mrs Shaw paced around the centre of the room. Now that they were finally at the hospital, both of them had time to feel the tension and exhaustion of what they'd been through in the last two hours. Now it was Mrs Shaw's turn for tears to fill her eyes. Helen stood up, and held on tight to her mother. They had never needed each other more than they did at this moment.

"You know, your idea about lifting the tree with the rope may have saved your Dad's life," Mrs Shaw said quietly.

"I don't think it was my idea. It just came to me at the right time." Her mother knew what she meant.

They stood still for several minutes, trying to let the fears subside. Then Mrs Shaw straightened, feeling a little better. "I think every muscle in my body hurts. After pulling on that rope, my arms must be two inches longer than they used to be," she added with a hint of a smile.

Helen smiled back. "You should see yourself. You've got twigs in your hair."

"Who's talking? You've got a leaf behind one ear, and from head to foot you're covered in mud."

There was a small mirror on the wall, and Helen moved over to look at herself. Her appearance was dreadful. She began to laugh, then to cry, and after a moment she couldn't distinguish between the two. Mrs Shaw began to laugh as well.

The nurse who came in right then with their cups of tea could make no sense of these two tree-like, mud splattered women, who didn't seem to be able to stop laughing. Working in the casualty department was a strange experience, and it got stranger all the time.

* * * *

They seemed to be in that small room forever.

Another nurse came in at one point to explain that X-rays were being taken of Mr Shaw because they could not tell externally how badly his head and chest were injured. When she left, Helen and her mother sat in silence. With little else to do, all kinds of frightening thoughts filled their minds. They couldn't even know if Mr Shaw would live.

At last the door opened, and a man in a white coat entered, introducing himself as the doctor who had been examining Mr Shaw. "There's encouragement and discouragement," he reported. "We were worried about all sorts of things. Mr Shaw could have had a fractured skull, a broken spine, and internal bleeding. Thankfully, our tests seem to indicate that none of these have happened." He paused to allow that news to sink in.

"So, how is he?" Mrs Shaw asked after a moment.

"Both legs are broken, and so is one rib. Those will heal. Our main worry still is that he has not regained consciousness. He must have had an almighty blow on his head, and until he comes round it's hard to be sure how well or hurt he really is."

"Will he be alright?" Mrs Shaw asked.

"As I've said, it's too early to be sure. But stay hopeful." He stood up to leave.

"Can we see him?" Helen asked.

The doctor hesitated. "Yes, okay, but it can be only for a minute."

He led them along a short corridor which had curtains on one side, each screening off a different area for treatment. Helen glanced through tiny cracks, and saw nurses bending over patients lying on beds raised high. She wondered what was wrong with each of these people. They turned a corner, and the doctor stopped. "I should warn you that because Mr Shaw is so weak, we've connected up various pieces of equipment to check his condition and to help him along. It looks a lot more frightening than it is." Both of them nodded, and he took them into a small room.

Mr Shaw lay still on the bed, with a nurse gently wiping his face to clean him up. Even though she'd been warned, Helen drew in her breath sharply when she saw her father more clearly. There seemed to be tubes and wires everywhere, connected up to various bottles or small machines. One was attached by a needle to his arm, while another went in by his nose. Wires ran to his chest where they joined small pads stuck there. He had a mask over his mouth, hissing as air went in and out.

"Don't worry about this equipment," the doctor said. "Some of it is keeping a check on things like his heart rate and blood pressure. And we're helping him breathe, not because he couldn't do it on his own, but to allow him to rest for now. I don't think we'll need all this for long."

Helen hoped he was right. Her Mum had crept quietly alongside her husband, and laid her hand gently on his arm. Helen moved to her side, and held her Dad's bruised fingers. No-one said anything out loud, but Helen guessed her Mum was praying like she was.

A moment later, and it was time to go.

"Can we wait in the hospital until he comes round?" Mrs Shaw asked the nurse.

"Of course, if that's what you'd like to do."

"We'd like to be near at hand as soon as he comes round."

The doctor joined in the conversation. "I think that may still take a little while. Could I suggest you might go home briefly..." He hesitated, trying to choose his words carefully. "That will give you a chance to change your clothes and have a brief rest. Then you can come back later."

Both Helen and her mother had temporarily forgotten their appearance. They couldn't easily be comfortable as they were. "If you think he's alright at the moment..?" Mrs Shaw said.

"His condition is quite stable just now," the doctor said comfortingly. "The nurse will be by his side every moment."

Mrs Shaw nodded. "We'll be back as soon as we can manage it."

Wearily Helen and her mother walked back along the corridor. "We've no car here, and I don't think either of us has the strength to walk," Mrs Shaw said.

She was about to add that they would somehow have to afford a taxi, when a friendly voice broke in. "Hi Helen. What are you doing here? Goodness, you look in a real mess." It was Wendy.

"Thanks for the compliment," Helen replied drily. In as few words as she could manage, she explained what had happened. Wendy, instantly realising how serious things were, managed to stay quiet and listen.

"Right," she said when Helen stopped. "My Dad will give you both a lift home."

"Is he here?"

"Yes, he's just along the way a bit, collecting Mum. Don't you remember? She works part-time as a nurse here, and she was on the early shift this morning, due to finish about now. We've come in to fetch her. But there will be no problem about taking you home as well."

Five minutes later and they were all on their way. The streets were far from busy because the wind still howled. Most people were keeping indoors.

"Is there anything else I can do for you right now?" Wendy's father asked as he pulled up in front of the Shaw's home.

"I don't think so," Mrs Shaw said. "We'll only be getting changed and then we'll be heading back to the hospital in our own car. But I'm so grateful for your help."

"If you're sure...?" he said.

"I'm sure. Thank you so much."

"Give me a call later, Helen," said Wendy. "I want to know how your Dad is."

"I'll do it from a call box at the hospital," she replied. "Our phone line came down with the tree."

Wendy and her parents moved off, leaving Helen and her mother to go indoors. Mrs Shaw flopped momentarily in a huge chair, exhaustion and strain written all over her face. "I'll make a cup of tea," Helen said, knowing her mother's needs.

"That would be good," she agreed.

A few minutes later, and Helen was back with the cup of tea. Her mother was fast asleep. Helen laid the tea beside her on a small table, and crept out.

Chapter 12

The doctor's words had lifted the blanket of fear from Helen and her mother. Their journey back to the hospital late in the afternoon was still difficult, but they felt ready to cope with whatever news they were given when they got there.

The receptionist in the casualty department, told them to take a seat while she called the appropriate nurse. A moment later and they were being ushered along the corridor. "You've come at the perfect moment, Mrs Shaw," the nurse said. "Your husband regained consciousness just a few minutes ago. He's very weak, but he's able to communicate quite well."

Helen's heart leapt, and she guessed her mother felt the same burst of excitement for her step quickened. Before she opened the door for them, the nurse explained that they'd taken off the oxygen mask temporarily to allow Mr Shaw to speak, but that all the other tubes were still there and that they couldn't stay too long in case they tired him. "We'll be careful," Mrs Shaw assured her as they stepped into the room.

Helen hung back a little behind her mother, not wanting to get in the way. Her father lay as he had before, but he was able to turn his head in their direction, and give a weak smile. Mrs Shaw picked up his hand and gripped it as tightly as she dared. "I don't remember coming here," he said quietly.

"No, I don't suppose you would," Mrs Shaw said. "But you certainly came quickly. It seemed like the ambulance had been fitted with a jet engine."

"Hello Dad," said Helen, as she came closer. He smiled lovingly at her.

"It's good to see you, my special daughter. I'm glad you're here too."

"I'm sorry about the accident. It was my fault for going off to church, and leaving you."

"No, no, no," he said slowly, and as firmly as he could. "You do talk a lot of nonsense sometimes Helen. You're not to blame at all."

"You rest just now," Mrs Shaw butted in. "We'll come back and see you in a little while."

He nodded. They turned to go, but Helen stopped half way to the door, went back to her father, and kissed him gently on the forehead. "I'm so glad you're alright Dad."

"Don't you worry yourself. Just keep praying for me as well as for your puppy."

Helen moved away, and she and her mother left the room. The nurse came with them for a moment. "Can we see him again this evening?" Mrs Shaw asked.

"That'll be fine. Come back whenever you like."

"Thank you for everything you're doing," Mrs Shaw said gratefully.

"Glad to help," the nurse said. "By the way, if you're staying around you might like to know that there's a small cafeteria open at this time. It's very reasonably priced, and you might want something to keep you going."

Neither Helen nor her mother had thought much about food, but the nurse's idea seemed good. "Especially if it's 'very reasonably priced'," Helen said, quoting the nurse with a smile. They soon found the cafeteria, collected a roll and cup of tea each, and sat down at a table.

"Dad mentioned the puppy," Helen said. "It may seem strange, but I've hardly thought about Sam since we came back from church."

Mrs Shaw sipped her tea. "It's typical of your father not to be thinking of his own problems, even at a time like this."

"Sam, what's going to happen to Sam?" Helen wondered out loud. "It still matters Mum, even though I know it's too late now. Dad getting well matters even more though."

Her Mum put her hand over Helen's and gave it a squeeze. "Given up believing...?" she asked. "All things are possible, you know."

* * * *

"It must have been around 11.30 a.m. I'd gone through to the kitchen to make coffee. All I remember was a huge gust of wind rattling the windows, followed by a loud crack from the tree." Mr Shaw concentrated, trying to recall what had happened earlier that day. "I knew what that meant. Any second the tree was going to fall. I didn't want to be in that kitchen with a tree coming through the roof, so I made a dash for it out the side door. After that I don't know what happened."

"We know the answer to that," Mrs Shaw said. "Somehow that tree didn't land on the house. Perhaps the gust of wind pushed it a little sideways. Anyway, it came down on you."

Mr Shaw raised his hand and touched his head. "Wood met wood, I think."

Helen joined in. "You must be pretty tough. I suppose they made them like that in the old days."

"Tough enough, you cheeky young lady," her father said.

"You must have been lying under that tree for nearly half an hour before we found you," Mrs Shaw said. "I shudder to think what might have happened if the church service hadn't been cut really short. We might have been easily another hour before coming home. From what the ambulanceman said, that hour would have been one too many."

They talked on for a while, but Mr Shaw was still far from well. Although he'd been given pain killers, he felt very sore from the broken bones and the blow on the head. After another few minutes, Mrs Shaw decided it was time that she and Helen said goodbye.

"Just get well and come home soon," Helen said.

"I'll do that," her Dad replied. "And Helen," he added, "have a happy birthday tomorrow."

Helen had completely forgotten about her birthday. There had been far too many other things to think about. Through most of the week, it had been Sam, and today it had been her Dad. "I'll try," she called back. "And

I'll be in to see you as soon as I can."

"Thanks for the warning," he replied, managing a good natured smile as she left the room.

Her mother held back a moment to have the last word alone with her husband. "I'll go on to the hallway and phone Wendy from a callbox," Helen said. "You can find me there." Mrs Shaw nodded.

Ten minutes later and Helen and her mother were heading home. "Wendy sounded relieved that Dad will be alright. She dashed off to tell her parents, forgetting I was having to put coins in to talk to her."

Mrs Shaw smiled. "Maybe it would help our family finances if we had a payphone installed at home...? It would be a way of reminding you how much calls cost!"

"I don't think that would be a good idea at all," said Helen, shaking her head resolutely. "Anyway," she went on, anxious to get off the subject of phone costs, "Wendy and her parents all send us their love."

"That's good of them. They're a kind family."

Mrs Shaw drove on silently. For a few minutes each of them was engrossed in her own thoughts. Helen eventually broke the silence. "Dad's doing really well. I hope he won't have to be in hospital long."

"I don't think so. The nurse said he'll be there for at least a few days, and then if everything's fine they'll let him out - probably in a wheelchair at first. He'll hate that, but it's better that he gets home as soon as possible."

Helen nodded in agreement. She didn't like the thought of her father not being with them. Her mind flipped back to her conversations with Wendy about fathers going away, and Helen was even more glad than ever that her Dad was normally at home.

Darkness had fallen by the time they reached the house. Mrs Shaw stood looking at the fallen tree for a moment, still with ropes attached and dangling over the chimney stack. There was nothing to be done about the tree or the ropes that night. The wind blew its chill through her bones. "Let's get inside, Helen," she said shivering. "At least since the tree is already down, it can't fall again. There's no reason why you can't sleep in your own room tonight."

"I'm glad of that," Helen replied. "I feel so tired." She yawned. "It seems as though today has lasted for ever."

"Just a few things have happened I suppose..." her mother conceded. "And Sunday is supposed to be the day of rest!"

They still didn't feel like having much to eat, but Mrs Shaw prepared a sandwich for each of them, and Helen opted for some warm milk to go with it. Within an hour of getting home, Helen had said goodnight to her mother and gone upstairs.

She wanted simply to flop down on her bed, but she knew that if she did she'd lie there for ages, when what she really needed to do was go to bed properly. Dogged with weariness, she had to force her body through the motions of getting ready. Her legs and arms still hurt from running and pulling. It seemed to take forever just to drag off her clothes.

Finally she reached the point when she could turn off the light. Her body willed her to climb under the bedclothes and shut her eyes. Instead, she made herself kneel at the side of the bed to pray.

"Lord, I don't think this is a night for long prayers," she said quietly. "First, I want to thank you for saving my Dad today. I don't know why you allowed that accident to happen, but I know you were helping rescue him. I thank you from the bottom of my heart, and I pray you'll be at his side in hospital and make him well soon."

Helen paused. There was one thing more to pray. "And God, I know I haven't got the money I need to save Sam, so I have to accept that he'll die tomorrow. Yet…" she hesitated, trying to make her words match her heart honestly. "I still believe he's meant to live and be mine. It's going to take an awful big miracle now, but if it's right, please do it. If it's not, please help me to cope."

She crawled from the floor into her bed. At any other time she might have lain awake worrying about her father, or about Sam. But not tonight. She wasn't even aware of her head going down on the pillow, she was asleep that fast.

Chapter 13

Eyes aching with the light, Helen struggled into wakefulness. Sleep had been a warm cocoon, and she would have preferred to stay in its peaceful and pleasant tranquillity. But a new day was forcing itself on her, and she had to wake up.

'What time is it?' she wondered. The wind seemed to be blowing its heart out still, but otherwise the weather had improved. The sun was shining, particularly brightly for early in the morning, Helen thought. She reached for her clock. "10.00 a.m.!" she said out loud. "I've been asleep for…" she did a quick calculation. "Over twelve hours!" Helen fell back on the bed. "I must have been tired," she said, and smiled.

But the smile didn't last. "Sam, poor Sam…is he still alive, or has he died already?" Helen spoke slowly, the very thought of a young puppy being put to death gnawing at her heart. "Why did he have to die?" she asked herself. "And on my birthday…?"

She got dressed, but not quickly. This was the first birthday she hadn't enjoyed. Normally she would be up almost before daylight, drag her parents out of bed, and pull them downstairs so that she could open whatever presents were for her. Not today. Her father was in hospital; the puppy she had believed was meant to be hers was dead. Being twelve simply wasn't enough to tip the balance in favour of feeling good.

"Well hello, and happy birthday Helen," her mother greeted her when she finally came downstairs. "For a while I wondered if you were going to sleep through your whole birthday. Are you ready for some breakfast?"

"Yes thanks," Helen replied. "I just didn't waken up until a short while ago."

"I had a pretty good sleep myself," her Mum said, and suddenly had to stifle a yawn. "I don't think I should still be tired!"

Helen sat down at the kitchen table, while her mother handed over a bowl of cereal, toast, and a cup of tea. "This looks like a lot of cereal," Helen said.

"An extra helping today because it's your birthday," her Mum responded cheerily. "Anyway, you're twelve, and getting bigger."

"I don't want to get big in the wrong direction," Helen retorted but with a smile. She munched her way into the cereal, and her Mum found a seat across the table from her.

"I wonder how your Dad slept...?" she said. "As soon as I came down this morning I picked up the phone to give the hospital a call to find out. I stood there for ages wondering why I couldn't hear a dial tone before I remembered the line was broken." Her face looked forlorn.

"When are we going to see him?" Helen asked.

"I decided to let you sleep as long as you wanted, and

then to go as soon as we were ready. Although, you may want to open your presents and cards before we set off."

Helen shook her head. "I'm not feeling much like it, Mum. I'll maybe not bother until later."

Her mother frowned. "You're upset about Sam, aren't you?"

Helen nodded. "I can't see why he had to die at all, and I can't understand why God let me believe I was to have him when he knew all along that that wouldn't happen."

Mrs Shaw's brow furled. "I don't understand it either, Helen. Although you must remember that we always said it would only be clearly right for you to have a puppy if the whole £50 came in time to buy him. And it hasn't…" She reached her hand to take Helen's. "Try not to be too disappointed today, and spoil your birthday."

Helen heaved a deep sigh. "I'll try. You've got enough worries and problems without me adding to them. At least Dad seems to be alright."

"Yes, I'm sure he's going to be fine. And after we've seen him I'll try and make a start on all the other things which have to be sorted out, like getting our phone line mended and arranging for someone to cut up this tree and remove it. There's plenty to do."

Helen stretched her body, trying to loosen muscles still tight and sore from the previous day's exertions. She forced a smile. "I'm glad today is a school holiday. I don't think I could have coped with being in classes after all the drama of yesterday." She hesitated. "And because of Sam…" she added quietly.

"I know," Mrs Shaw said. "We'll get through this day together somehow, won't we?"

* * * *

Fifteen minutes later and they were ready to go. The few breakfast dishes were washed, hairstyles were reasonably in order, and coats were on. "The wind is still strong, but thankfully it's not a full blown storm like Saturday and Sunday," Helen said, looking out the window.

"And we've no trees left to blow down...," her Mum added philosophically. "Okay, have you got everything you need?"

"I don't think I need anything, so I guess I have."

They moved towards the door. "Oh, I'm the one who's forgetful. It'll help if I take the car keys," said Mrs Shaw.

"I haven't learned enough about crime to know how to start the engine without them," teased Helen.

"Now where did I leave them...?" her mother murmured, walking back through to the kitchen. "Helen," she called. "Have you seen the keys anywhere?"

"No, but I'll help you look. Aren't they in one of the kitchen drawers as usual?"

"They don't seem to be. I was so tired last night, I probably laid them down anywhere. Well, since we drove home we can be confident they must be somewhere here."

"Hmm..." Helen said quietly, thinking it wiser not to mention any of the impolite thoughts which flashed through her brain.

Drawers were emptied, cushions pulled from chairs, flower pots examined, pockets turned inside out. After ten minutes the car keys still couldn't be found. Helen ran her hands down the crack at the side of the seat cushions of the sofa. Mrs Shaw ransacked her bedroom in case she'd taken the keys in there. Still they remained stubbornly lost. Twenty minutes had elapsed.

"Could you have dropped them outside the front door?" Helen asked.

"I think I'd have heard them fall," her mother replied. "But we'd better check."

Both headed out of the door, and began to scour the ground between the car and the house. The wind was blowing the dust in small whirlpools, and it soon got in their eyes as they bent low to search. "This is terrible," Mrs Shaw said. "I'm sorry Helen. I'd lose my head if it wasn't screwed on tight." Helen smiled. It was funny to hear her mother say out loud one of the thoughts she'd bitten back twenty minutes earlier.

Their concentration on scanning every inch of ground was suddenly interrupted by a voice. "Someone must have lost a diamond ring if you're looking that closely!" Their heads bobbed up. It was the postman.

"Phew...," Mrs Shaw said. "You gave us quite a fright."

"I'm sorry to do that. There's just a couple of letters today, or could they be birthday cards addressed to a young lady...?"

"They could be," Helen answered, her face flushing red with embarrassment as she took the envelopes from his hand.

"Well, many happy returns! I'm sorry to be a little late this morning. It's still difficult getting to some of the homes on my round because of debris from the storm." He glanced at the fallen tree. "You look as though you've experienced a bit of that yourself."

"Yes we have," said Mrs Shaw. "Perhaps I'll tell you the full story another day, but at this moment we're rather stuck because we've lost the car keys. Right now they're almost as valuable as diamonds to us because we can't go anywhere without them."

The postman glanced around. "So how did you manage to open your car?" he asked.

"It's not open," Mrs Shaw said, but then she looked more closely. "Oh! It *is* open. How can it be unlocked without the keys...?"

"One way," the postman said cheerily, "is if you didn't lock it in the first place." He walked over to the driver's side of the car. "I know where your keys are!" he laughed.

Mrs Shaw hurried round, and looked where he pointed. "Not still in the ignition?! What a doddery old fool I am." She looked thoroughly exasperated with herself. "Helen, I am sorry for all this fuss. Last night I simply wasn't thinking very straight, and only wanted to get inside the house."

"That's okay Mum," Helen said. "There's no harm done. Our car's still here, and we've got the keys now."

"Thank you for your help," Mrs Shaw said to the postman.

"Happy to oblige," he said. "I hope the rest of your day goes more smoothly."

"I hope so too," Mrs Shaw muttered as she watched him retreat down the lane. "At last we can get going Helen. By the way, who are your cards from?"

Helen had almost forgotten she was holding the envelopes. She studied the outside of each. "This first one is from Wendy. I recognise that scrawl of hers, and it's got a local postmark." She screwed her eyes up as she studied the second envelope. "I don't know about this one. The postmark is blurred, and I don't know the handwriting. Any guesses Mum?" Her mother looked at it. She stiffened up a little, as if a thought had come to her. "Let me see it more closely a moment." Helen handed it to her mother, who peered at it in a curious way. "I think I do know who it's from," she said mysteriously, "but you'll have to open it before I can be sure."

Helen hadn't planned to open either of them immediately, but her mother's strange look and odd tone of voice made her want to find out who had sent the card. She edged her finger beneath the flap of the envelope, and tore it backwards trying carefully not to destroy the contents. Out came a birthday card, a short letter, and another smaller envelope. Helen looked first at the card.

"It's from your Great Aunt Bertie, isn't it?" asked Mrs Shaw.

Helen nodded.

"We haven't heard from her for years," her mother went on. "I don't think she's ever sent you a birthday card before. In fact, you've probably met her only two or three times. Why would she send you a card this time?"

Helen had begun to read the letter. As her eyes moved down the page, the colour drained from her cheeks.

"Helen! Helen! Are you alright?" asked her Mum, seeing her daughter going rigid and looking as though she would faint any second.

"I don't believe it. I don't believe it," Helen said. She clutched the second, smaller envelope tightly. "It can't be true, not now."

"What's not true? What does the letter say Helen?"

"Let me read it to you," Helen said forming her words in a very deliberate manner in order to control herself. "She says, 'Dear Helen, You will be perfectly well aware that it is not my custom to send gifts at birthdays. However, the other day I happened to glance a few pages ahead in my book of dates and noticed your birthday was on Monday.

Ever since then I have not been able to get it out of my head that this year I ought to send you something. I have even wakened up in the middle of the night thinking about it. I cannot feel at peace until I put this card and gift in the post to you.

If you look in the small envelope you will find a brand new £20 note. It's for you. I hope you have a good birthday. Yours sincerely, Great Aunt Bertie.' Mum..." Helen said, her voice quivering with excitement. "Mum, the money...!" She tore open the small envelope, and there was the new banknote her great aunt had promised. Tears poured from Helen's eyes as she struggled to get the rest of the words out. "Mum...the rest of the money has come."

Mrs Shaw was almost as overcome as Helen. Almost mechanically, she lifted the letter from Helen's hand, and read it all through again. Helen simply stood staring at the £20 note. "There's another message at the end," Mrs Shaw said in a dream like voice. "'P.S., Don't expect anything next year.' That's just like Bertie."

"Do you think," Helen broke in, "that there's any chance Sam could still be alive?"

"Oh Helen, no, I don't." Mrs Shaw looked at her watch. "It's well after eleven. The people at the cat and dog home told me last week that they would be putting Sam down first thing on Monday morning. I'm sorry..."

"There must be a chance," Helen said desperately. She clenched her teeth, and closed her eyes. "There must be a chance," she repeated. "I have believed this puppy is right for me, and now God has put the last piece in place to allow that to happen. It can't be too late."

"We'll phone and see," said her Mum. "Oh no, the phone line is broken. How frustrating!"

"We've got to go there. We've got to go there...now!"

Chapter 14

"Right, fetch the rest of the money and get in the car. Let's get moving." Mrs Shaw could be very authoritative when she needed to be. "If there's any way of saving this dog, let's take it,' she added as she settled behind the wheel. Helen didn't need to be told twice. She ran indoors to collect the £30, then returned and jumped into the passenger seat.

Mrs Shaw turned the ignition key, the engine fired...and died. She pulled out the choke lever. "The air's cold, so the engine needs a little help." She turned the key again, and the starter motor cranked round and round, but this time the engine showed no signs of life at all.

"Come on Mum. We must go," said Helen.

"I'm trying," came the agitated reply.

Once more she switched the key to on. The engine turned over and over: six times, eight times, ten times. She tried again, blipping the accelerator peddle with her foot. There was plenty of noise, but the engine wouldn't start. Mrs Shaw switched off. "Perhaps the engine is a little damp after all the rain, or I may have flooded it accidentally with petrol."

"What do we do about it?" Helen asked, looking

more anxious than ever.

"I'm not really sure," her mother replied. "If your father was here, he'd know."

"We've got to do something!" Helen exploded. "We can't just sit here while Sam is put to death."

"Give it a minute, and I'll have another go." That minute felt like ten. Eventually Mrs Shaw reached for the key again, her hand trembling in fear that once more the car wouldn't start. "This time..." she said. "It's got to go."

She switched the key, the starter heaved round, and again, and again, but the engine refused to burst into life. Over and over the motor turned, until it began to lose some power, becoming slower and slower.

Mrs Shaw switched the key to off. "I think I'm draining the battery," she said. "This doesn't look good."

"Mum, it must start," Helen said bursting into tears. "It must, it must..."

"I can't risk it again at the moment. I'll have to wait."

"Then I'm going to run to the cat and dog home," Helen said desperately, climbing out of the car.

"Helen, it's three miles away. You can't run that far."

"What I can't do is stay here, knowing Sam's only chance of life is being lost by a car which won't go." Before her mother could say another word, Helen took to her heels and was off along the lane.

More slowly, Mrs Shaw got out of the car, and raised the bonnet over the engine. She looked at the mass of engine, pipes, and wires, and hadn't the first idea of what to do. She'd heard George talk sometimes about a damp distributor, but the only distributors she knew were those who put the free newspaper through their door every week.

"Lord God," she prayed almost silently, "I don't know if you're in the business of making car engines work, but if you are, here's one that needs the gift of life right now."

* * * *

Helen ran as fast as she could down the lane, feeling like she had just the day before. Then she was running to save her father. Now it was for Sam.

She turned into the road, heading towards town. She was as fit as anyone her age, but she'd set off at a speed she couldn't possibly keep up. Her lungs began to demand more air than she could suck in and blow out. Her cheeks puffed, her heart pounded, and her legs protested at the pain. 'I've got to keep going. I've got to get there to rescue Sam.' But her silent determination couldn't overcome the inevitable exhaustion which hit her like a wall after about a mile.

She had to halt, her head pounding and feeling dizzy through lack of air. Her body bent double, as stomach aches gripped her. A moment later and she forced her slim frame to start running again. "I've got to go on. I can't stop...not now," she told herself.

But a few hundred yards later and her pace slowed. Helen felt a dark cloud settle over her eyes, and she sensed herself weave from side to side unsteadily.

Instinctively she reached out to balance herself, scraping her hand painfully against a stone wall. She lurched into the wall, crying with pain and helplessness, half standing, half slumped and totally unable to move.

Into her befuddled and angry mind came the sound of a car horn, blasting noisily over and over again. She wrenched her head to the side, screwing her eyes tight to try and evaporate the misty cloud in front of them. Helen saw the outline of a car on the other side of the road. As she tried to focus on it, she heard a voice she knew. "Helen, over here. Come on! The car's going now." It was her mother.

A burst of energy surged back into her body. She crossed the road, and pulled herself into the passenger seat. Then they were off, driving through the busy streets of the town.

"How did you get the car started?" asked Helen when she was able to speak again.

"All I did was look at the engine, wait a few minutes, and then try again. This time it went. Maybe there was outside assistance," her mother replied mysteriously.

Helen didn't probe any further. "Faster Mum, faster!"

"There's a speed limit in town, Helen."

"Yes, but this is life and death."

Her mother squeezed another mile or two per hour out of the engine, but refused to press the accelerator peddle any harder. "Apart from whether it's right or wrong, if I go too fast I could run someone down. That's also a matter of life and death."

Helen grimaced. She didn't like any delay, but she

couldn't argue. Mrs Shaw did her best to weave in and out of the traffic, and found a shortcut which avoided one busy street. "Traffic lights ahead," she murmured, "and they're at green..." But almost as if they saw her coming, the lights switched to red. There was no choice but to brake.

Helen's stomach began to churn with panic as they waited. "Come on... come on... Change!" The lights persisted on red. "They must be stuck, Mum."

"Patience, Helen. They'll change. Just wait."

Helen saw the light for the traffic on the other road switch to red. "Right, we're going," she warned her mother. But they weren't. Pedestrian lights came on, and there was another minute of agonized waiting before finally Mrs Shaw got the green for go.

Somehow they seemed to get behind every bus in town, each content to idle its way along as if its timetable had been abolished. They tried another shortcut along some back streets, only to be halted by a workman directing a large articulated lorry as it took six attempts to reverse into a factory gate. More anguished seconds were spent at road works, when the man directing traffic seemed to have his red 'STOP' sign fixed in their direction. Helen felt as if her heart was pounding more while seated in the car than it had when she was running down the road.

At last they were there, turning into the gates of the cat and dog home. There was one building near the entrance, and behind it rows of smaller sheds containing kennels. There were high walls, and gates separating different areas. The car's brakes screeched loudly as Mrs Shaw raced the car into a parking space.

Even inside the car they could hear the loud noise of countless dogs all barking. "We just mustn't be too late," Helen shouted, as she flung the car door open and raced towards the reception building.

Mrs Shaw was no more than a metre behind her daughter as a swing door was swept aside. Inside was a corridor, and near the end they could see a sign saying 'Enquiries'. They ran to a sliding glass window below the sign. Helen knocked loudly on the window. Inside the office was one elderly lady secretary, busy writing in a large book. "Just a moment," she called without looking up.

Beads of sweat began to break out on Helen's forehead. Delay was something with which she simply could not cope at this moment. She knocked again on the window. The secretary was unmoved. "Just wait please," she said, her voice muffled through the glass.

After what seemed an age, she laid down her pen, carefully closed the book, and rose from her chair to come to the window. She undid a latch, and slid the glass along. "I'm sorry to have kept you. How can I help?"

"I'm here for Sam," Helen blurted out. "Sam, my puppy..."

"Sam...?" The secretary reached over for another large book. "I don't remember entering a puppy by that name."

Mrs Shaw interrupted. "No, you won't have him by that name. He's a little fellow with brown floppy ears. My daughter found him, and he was brought in here by the police not last Saturday but the one before."

"I see," came the reply. "Now, what date would that be?" The secretary reached over to look at a calendar pinned to the wall. Her finger traced along the numbers. She seemed to take forever, and Helen shifted her weight from foot to foot in agitation. She closed her eyes and bit her tongue to avoid saying the wrong thing. "It must have been the fourteenth," concluded the secretary. "I'll check my register of admissions. Just wait a moment."

She moved back to her desk, and began to turn the pages of the large book in which she had been writing earlier. Each page was turned from right to left with just one hand, as if the register was a valuable historical document. "This is taking forever," Helen whispered angrily to her mother. "She's got to hurry up."

Thankfully the secretary seemed to find the right page at that moment. "Oh yes, there were only two dogs brought in that day. One was an old black dog, found scavenging behind a restaurant in town. The other was a small puppy found in a lane just on the outskirts. So, you're asking about the puppy, are you?"

Helen sighed deeply, trying so hard to control herself. "That's right," she said forcefully. "We want to buy the puppy."

"Well let me see what's become of him," responded the secretary. "My other book will tell me that." She moved back to the counter beside the window, reaching down to a shelf and pulling out another large volume. Then began the same painstaking procedure of turning pages one by one. Eventually she reached the appropriate page, and ran her finger down the lines.

The suspense was too much for Helen. "Where is he?" she asked desperately.

"I'm just checking, my dear," the secretary responded. Her finger rested on the last line. "Oh," she said, her voice slowing, "that's right. I only wrote this entry earlier this morning. I'm so very sorry. I'm afraid the puppy you're asking about was...em, I fear he..." her words petered out.

"He was put to death?" The question came straight from the deepest fear in Helen's heart.

"I'm afraid he was."

An icy numbness gripped Helen's mind and body. There wasn't a word to say. In a daze, she allowed her mother to take her gently by the arm and walk her back up the corridor, out of the building, and to their car.

Chapter 15

"I'm sorry Helen. We tried our best. It's over now."
Mrs Shaw knew there were no right words to say. She could only try to comfort her daughter. "I wish with all my heart this had never happened, especially on your birthday."

Helen said nothing. Mrs Shaw wasn't surprised at that, since she must be feeling devastated with disappointment. It was a peculiarly cruel twist for Helen to get the money she needed just too late to save the puppy. Grimly, Mrs Shaw shook her head in puzzlement, unlocked the car doors, and both climbed inside.

"Suppose we go and get a coffee, and maybe a bar of chocolate to cheer us up?" Mrs Shaw said. "We could do with something special at the moment." She started the car and crunched the gear lever into reverse.

"Stop! We can't go." It was Helen, her voice agitated, filled with alarm.

"Pardon Helen? What do you mean?"

"I mean the lady in the office is wrong. All week I've believed that puppy would be mine. You said it would be right if the money came. And it has. She must be wrong."

"Helen, Helen…she's not wrong. It was down in her book that Sam died earlier this morning. We have to face the fact that we're simply too late." Mrs Shaw looked with concern at Helen. "You can't cling to wishful thinking. You must let the idea go."

"No! She's wrong. Mum, we've got to go back and make her check."

"Check? She'll think we're mad."

"Please…we must check!" Helen's words and face pleaded for action.

Mrs Shaw shrugged her shoulders. "Okay," she said, switching off the car engine. "I hope we don't annoy her…" She didn't relish that prospect, but if checking up helped Helen to accept the inevitable, it would be worth it.

Together they strode back down the long corridor, and again Helen rapped on the window. The secretary looked up, and gave a quizzical look when she saw the same two faces back again. She opened the sliding window.

"I'm so very sorry to bother you any more," Mrs Shaw said in her most apologetic tone of voice. "We just wonder if there could be any possibility of a mistake."

"There is no mistake," replied the secretary huffily. "I keep a strict record of what happens with every cat and dog which comes into this home. The puppy you were asking about was on the list to be put down this morning, and that was done much earlier. I'm sorry to have to give you that news.

"Is there no chance he might still be alive…?" asked

Helen sadly. "I know he's meant to be mine." Helen's face had sincerity and disappointment written across it in huge letters.

The secretary looked at her, and her tone softened. "I wish I had some other message to give you, young lady. I'm sure the puppy meant a great deal to you." She paused, and after a moment added, "If it helps, you can go through the gate at the back here, and across the main yard to find Frank. He's in charge of the dog section today, and he'll confirm what I've told you."

"Thank you!" said Helen quickly, and she was off out of the door to the rear. "Come on Mum, hurry up!" she called over her shoulder. "There's maybe still time."

Mrs Shaw shook her head in mild despair. This was only extending the agony, and besides, she wasn't built for running... They hurried to the main fence around the kennels. The gate was firmly shut.

"It's okay, it's only fastened with a latch," Helen said, fiddling with a heavy ring of metal which had been pulled over a metal hook. She prised it off, and ran at top speed into the yard. Both of them scanned all around. There were several more gates leading to different areas.

"Which way?" Helen shouted.

"I don't know," came the exasperated reply from her mother. "The secretary said to go across the main yard, but she didn't say in which direction."

Helen stood absolutely still. A second later she pointed to one of the gates at the far right hand corner. "It's that way," she said confidently.

"How do you know?"

"I can't explain. I just know," Helen replied as she started running again.

It was about thirty metres to the next fence. Helen outran her mother, and began to try to unlatch the gate. Her mother puffed into place behind her. "This one's more tricky...it seems to be jammed," said Helen grimly, using as much force as she could to haul the ring off its hook.

Mrs Shaw was looking beyond the gate. "Helen," she said suddenly. "Look..."

Helen glanced at her mother, and then turned her eyes to follow her mother's pointing hand. There, fifty metres beyond where they stood behind the wire fence, was a man carrying a small, floppy eared brown dog, its bright eyes peering out from his arms. "That's Sam," Helen murmured. Then more loudly, "Mum! That's Sam!"

But, even as she was realising that, things were happening which temporarily struck both of them dumb. The man reached a small, kennel sized container. With one hand he slid upwards a doorway on the front, and gently eased the dog inside. He paused there only for a moment.

The man's hand lowered the door. As he did so, Helen and her mother saw a notice fastened to the door. In large letters were the words, 'DANGER! LIVE ELECTRICITY'. It was the Hulec Chamber!

"STOP! STOP! Helen shouted through the gate. "STOP! THAT'S MY DOG!"

Remembering the attendant's name, Mrs Shaw

shouted with her. "STOP! FRANK! DON'T KILL HIM!" They shouted more loudly, voices crackling with the strain. "STOP! STOP! STOP!" But Frank's left hand moved towards a large red button to the side of the container.

"FRANK! NO! NO!" they screamed.

Mrs Shaw sagged back, lowering her voice. "It's no good Helen," she said. "He can't hear us for the wind."

Stunned into terrified silence, they stood behind their wire fence, and watched the man's hand strike the red button firmly, and hold it pressed down.

"Sam's dead," Helen said quietly. As tears streamed down her face, Helen turned away, and buried her head in her mother's arms.

Chapter 16

Helen felt dizzy and sick. Seconds earlier the adrenaline had been pumping round her body at what seemed like a 100 miles per hour. Now, every ounce of energy had been stripped from her. She held on to her mother, eyes wet with tears, her heart seared with pain and sadness. "This might help you," said Mrs Shaw, handing her a white handkerchief. "Try and dry your eyes."

Helen had little success, but she stood back and gazed up at her Mum's concerned face. Her voice broke as she tried to speak. "Why did it all have to end like this?"

"I don't know," replied Mrs Shaw wearily. "I just don't know. Come on, let's go home."

She turned to leave, but Helen looked wistfully over those last few metres to the container where her puppy had died. "Could I see Sam one last time?" she asked.

"I don't think that's a good idea, Helen."

"Please Mum."

"Are you sure?" Mrs Shaw looked more troubled. The situation was bad already. She didn't want to increase the risk of her twelve-year-old being left with even more unpleasant memories which would become nightmares. "He might not look...well, at his best now."

"Even so, I'm sure. I only want to say a final goodbye."

"Alright then."

At last the gate's ring finally yielded to upward force, and they made their way through the gate. Mrs Shaw kept her arm tightly round Helen's shoulders as together they walked across the few metres to where Frank stood. Just one minute earlier would have made all the difference, thought Mrs Shaw. It would have been enough if there had been only twenty metres instead of fifty between us and Frank. Then he'd have heard us. But she kept such thoughts to herself. Helen was already upset quite enough.

Frank was taken by surprise when he finally realised he had company. Startled he turned towards them. "Don't creep up on me like that," he said.

"Couldn't you hear us shouting?" asked Mrs Shaw.

"Hear you? How would I hear anyone when the wind's blowing and just about every dog in the place is barking? What were you shouting for anyway?"

Mrs Shaw shook her head sadly before answering. Helen stood still beside her, muffled sobs coming from behind the handkerchief she held to her face. "The dog you just put to death in there," she said pointing at the container. "We'd come for it."

"The little brown puppy? The one in there?" Frank asked, looking more surprised than ever.

"Yes. That one," replied Mrs Shaw, growing irritated with the situation and Frank's abrupt way of speaking. "Could my daughter be allowed to see his body for a moment? She would like the chance to say goodbye to him."

Frank laughed, and Mrs Shaw became really angry. "Excuse me, but this is no time to laugh." But Frank didn't seem able to stop his chortling. "If you continue I'll report you to the management of this home. Can't you see how upset my daughter is at this moment?"

"Oh yes, I can see. But I don't think she's going to be like that for very long," said Frank.

"I beg your pardon! What do you mean?"

"This is what I mean," Frank went on. He bent down, gripped the handle of the small door, and pulled it upwards. Light rushed into the container, and all three bent down to look inside. What they saw made Helen and her mother jump with fright. Two tiny eyes peered back at them. Then a tail wagged, ears flapped, and despite a few wires a very much alive little puppy called Sam scampered out and jumped up and down at Helen's feet.

"He's alive! He's alive! Mum, Sam's alive!" Helen burst into tears all over again, but didn't stop to wipe any of them away. In a second she had undone the electrodes and had her puppy scooped up in her arms. She held him tight, and Sam licked her face, clearing the tears with his tongue.

Mrs Shaw had gone pale. So many strange and unexpected things had happened that weekend she wouldn't have believed anything else could take her by surprise. But this did. "How!? Please explain," she said weakly, looking towards Frank.

"That's not difficult," he replied, and gave the container a kick. "It's the wretched electricity supply.

It keeps failing just when I need to get on with my work. All morning I've been fetching that puppy from his pen, putting him in this container, pressing the button…only to find there's no power. The cable has gone dead. I put him back in his pen, wait for the supply to be restored, bring him out, and then it fails again. What you saw just now was my fourth go at carrying out my orders. But yet again the power fails."

"It'll be because of the weekend storms," Mrs Shaw pondered. "Probably trees have been blown on to power lines and made the electricity supply unreliable. Or, maybe they have to switch the power off while they repair them."

Frank shrugged his shoulders. "Could be that's it." He looked at Helen holding Sam close, running her hands lovingly over his head and stroking his ears. With a laugh, he pointed one hand up towards the sky. "Whatever the technical explanation, someone up there must be watching over that little fellow."

Helen smiled; her mother smiled. And both exchanged glances which said, 'He's right'.

* * * *

The secretary in the office heard yet another sharp rap on the glass window. She glanced up from her books, and saw the two familiar faces of Helen and her mother waiting.

"Back again," she said, sliding the glass to one side. "I told you it was too late…" But even as she spoke, her words died on her lips. For there was the puppy which shouldn't have been alive, curled up in contented comfort in Helen's arms.

"You see, it wasn't too late. You were wrong," said Helen.

Normally Mrs Shaw would have corrected Helen for her bluntness, but this was no moment for scolding. Instead she couldn't help the feeling of inner satisfaction as the secretary struggled to find anything to say.

"I don't understand...this can't be, well it shouldn't be..." She was lost for words.

Frank came in at that moment. He'd taken a few minutes to lock gates and make sure the other dogs were secure. The secretary turned to him. "Frank, I told these people that this puppy had already been put down this morning. Why is it still alive?"

"Electricity failures," he said. "Otherwise he'd have been gone an hour and a half or two hours ago." He turned towards the two women, and added. "We always get the unpleasant jobs over with first thing, around 9.30 a.m. Mrs Entwhistle knows that, and writes down the names of those dogs in her book."

"That job is always done early," Mrs Entwhistle confirmed. "I've worked here for more than twenty years, and it's never once been any different. That's why I didn't have any doubts when you arrived so much later." She sighed, and sat down.

"Oh dear, that could have been such a terrible mistake. I'm so glad you came back to check."

Mrs Shaw took her turn to sigh. "We wouldn't have, if it had only been up to me." She turned towards Helen. "But there was someone else here with an awful lot of faith that Sam couldn't be dead. The trust - and persistence - of youth..."

"Great to be young," said Frank.

"Great to have faith," added Mrs Shaw.

"Great to have £50," murmured Helen.

Chapter 17

Helen was chattering away at a machine gun rate of fire to her father. She'd already given him the main news about Sam, and was moving on now to the finer details. "Dad, you just couldn't imagine how everything fitted together this morning."

Mr Shaw pulled himself into a more comfortable position in his hospital bed. "Try me," he said.

His daughter needed little encouragement. "Well we should have been away from home early to come and see you. If we'd done that, we wouldn't have been there when the postman came. But Mum lost her car keys and that delayed us. In fact it was the postman who found them. They were...er, still in the car, but I wasn't supposed to tell you that." Mr Shaw smiled. He was well used to his wife's forgetfulness.

"Then there was the card from Great Aunt Bertie with £20 inside. Imagine! Money from Great Aunt Bertie, of all people!? Anyway, that brought the total up to £50, and we just had to try to get to the home in time to save Sam. You should have seen Mum drive! Well, on second thoughts, maybe it's better that you didn't..."

And on Helen went, giving her father the benefit of

every last event, emotion, near tragedy, and then triumph. Fifteen minutes later she paused for breath. Her Dad took his chance. "Helen, hold it there!" he interjected. "You can save some of the story for another visit."

"But aren't you excited too?" asked Helen, looking anxious for a moment.

Mr Shaw laughed, and then clutched at his side. Laughing hurt! "Yes, I'm thrilled for you," he winced. "But maybe you should give your Mum a chance to come and see me as well today...?"

Helen gave a guilty grin. She'd abandoned her mother to puppy sitting duty in the car while she went into the hospital first to tell her Dad about Sam. Helen got up to leave. "Thanks for being so encouraging Dad," she said as she turned to go.

"Well," he replied thoughtfully, "I didn't doubt God would give you the right answer."

"He certainly did that," Helen agreed cheerily, heading for the door.

"And by the way," her Dad added, "happy birthday!"

"Oh yes! Thanks. I'd almost forgotten."

With another laugh, Helen was off along the corridor, hardly a care in the world.

Mrs Shaw was more than a little relieved to see Helen. Sam hadn't seemed to enjoy being in her company quite as much as with Helen. "Maybe you just don't have the right smell about you," Helen suggested.

Her mother frowned. She wasn't sure how to take that remark. Very readily she passed Sam over to Helen, and set off towards Mr Shaw's hospital ward.

Helen climbed inside the car, Sam on her knee. It felt so good to be there, just the two of them. "This is my own puppy," she said to herself, and then said it again simply because it sounded good. She ran her hand over his ears, and rubbed him gently under his chin. Sam knew what he wanted, though, and turned to lie on his back so that Helen would stroke his tummy.

A moment later and he was back on his four paws, standing as tall as he could to watch people passing by in the car park. "You're certainly interested in what's happening around you," Helen said to him. "We'll have plenty of time to explore together in the future. I know some great walks through woods that you're going to love." Sam licked her hand. Helen was sure he understood every word she said.

Another thought came to Helen, this one a little different. She bowed her head. "Lord," she prayed, "I don't know how you were able to make all this come out right. But you did, and I want to thank you for that. Thank you for keeping your promises, even when it seemed impossible."

She hadn't finished her prayer when there was a sharp knock on the window. Helen jumped at the noise, and jumped again when she saw a face peering in at her. "Wendy!" she exclaimed when she overcame her fright enough to recognise her friend. Helen wound down the car window. "You scared me half to death creeping up like that."

"I didn't mean to," Wendy said. "In fact I waved at you six times but you didn't seem to notice. Sometimes you seem to go around with your eyes closed."

Helen didn't enlighten her that the last remark was very close to the truth at that precise moment. "My Dad was giving Mum a lift to work so I came too, and recognised your car in the car park. I came over to say hello and happy birthday."

"Thanks," Helen said, opening the car door to step outside, Sam cradled safely in her arms. Now it was Wendy's turn to be startled. She hadn't seen Sam through the window. "Helen! It's a dog!"

"Very clever!" replied Helen with a touch of friendly sarcasm. "Wendy, I'd like you to meet Sam."

"You're kidding! You actually got him?"

"That's right. Just this morning, and only just in time."

"How? You didn't have enough money. I bet your Mum and Dad caved in at the last minute and gave it to you."

"No they didn't. They really didn't believe that was right. No, the money came this morning through the post from my Great Aunt Bertie. She's never sent anything before, but she wrote in a letter that she had to send £20 this year. She didn't know why, but she knew she had to do it. How about that for a miracle?"

"It must be the nearest I've ever come to one," said Wendy, looking both perplexed and impressed. "I can't understand it. A week ago you didn't have a penny, and there was no likelihood of getting any money. Now you have £50. Well, you had £50, and what you have now is Sam. That's beyond me..."

Helen plucked up her courage. "God is interested in Wendys as well as puppies. Maybe you should get to know God for yourself..."

"Maybe I should," Wendy replied thoughtfully. "Maybe I should..."

* * * *

"Your Dad is looking a lot better today, isn't he?" asked Mrs Shaw when she rejoined Helen at the car.

"Yes he is. When do you think he'll get out of hospital?"

"The doctor has said it'll probably be later on this week if he continues to improve. It'll be good to get him home." Mrs Shaw's voice betrayed some relief at that thought. "Okay, young lady, now it's time for us to get home." She turned the ignition key, and started the engine.

"Mum, I hate to ask this when we've so little money, but we'll need some things for Sam like a lead, a dog basket, and food! Could we go to the pet shop on the way?"

"No, I don't think we should do that." Her Mum's firmness surprised Helen.

"But he needs these things. We've got to get them."

"We can talk about that later." And before Helen could say another word, Mrs Shaw put the car into gear, and drove off.

Helen was silent most of the way home. She couldn't understand why her mother had been so reluctant to buy anything for Sam. 'Maybe the money situation is really bad,' she told herself. Nevertheless, her puppy needed food to eat and something in which to sleep. Meanwhile Helen sat quietly helping Sam stay calm. She wasn't sure how much of a memory young puppies had, but she knew that Sam's last car journey ten days earlier couldn't have been a good experience for him.

A few minutes later they drove up the lane to their house and parked outside. "Make me a cup of tea please, Helen. I've a couple of things I need to attend to in the back garden." Helen took Sam into the house, and let him sniff his way round the rooms while she filled the kettle and organised the tea.

"This is your new home Sam. You're going to be happy here. Don't you worry about anything. I'll look after you." Sam cocked his head to one side, as if he accepted Helen's reassuring words. The water boiled in the kettle, and Helen poured it into the teapot.

"The tea's ready," she called out of the window to her mother.

"I'll be right in." Sure enough, her mother appeared shortly. They moved through to their living room, and sat together sipping tea. "He seems happy," Mrs Shaw remarked, looking down at Sam who had curled up beside Helen's feet. "I don't suppose he found the cat and dog home very comfortable. I know they do their best there, but it can't be the same as being in a real home."

"And he's safe here," Helen added.

"Yes, he certainly is," Mrs Shaw agreed. "He's safe and wanted."

"Do you mean that Mum?" A hint of anxiety tinged Helen's words. "Do you and Dad not mind me having him?" It was a question she'd wanted to ask ever since her mother had refused to buy anything for Sam.

"Helen, we are delighted the money came in time, and at last you've got your own puppy."

Helen felt a wave of relief. "Thanks Mum," she said.

Mrs Shaw put down her tea cup. "What about these birthday presents you didn't feel like opening this morning?"

"Oh yes. I'd forgotten about them!"

"Come on then. There's a few parcels over there beside the piano. Why don't you see what's in them?"

Gently Helen dislodged Sam from her feet as she moved over to fetch her presents. She picked them up, feeling each carefully for some clue to what was inside. "Are these from you?" she asked.

"The first two are from Dad and me," Mrs Shaw said smiling.

"I could have guessed that," said Helen. "You always put a few extra layers of wrapping paper round your presents so I can't tell what's inside."

Mrs Shaw laughed. "You'll just have to open them to find out."

"I'm going to start with this heavy one," Helen announced, resuming her seat. Sam seemed grateful. Helen's foot made a good pillow for his head.

Helen began to ease the parcel apart, trying to preserve the colourful wrapping paper. Her self control couldn't last, though, and she soon began ripping the paper to get at what was inside. Finally the last layer came away. Helen's eyes bulged as she gazed at a superb ceramic dog bowl! She was speechless.

"Useful?" Mrs Shaw asked.

"Very useful," Helen managed to reply. "Thank you. It's exactly what Sam needs."

"On to the next one then," her mother urged.

This time Helen didn't even try to be careful with the paper. She wanted to know what was inside. "This one is lighter, and doesn't feel so solid," she said.

"Could be..." Mrs Shaw commented, giving little away.

Wrappers were strewn all over the floor by now, but finally Helen pulled the last piece of paper away. "A dog lead! And a pretty little collar for Sam!" She reached over to her Mum, and hugged her tight. "Thank you. Thank you so much."

"There's another present in with those," Mrs Shaw pointed out. "It's a little smaller though."

Helen had seen nothing, but then realised she had buried a tiny, round parcel among the debris. "It's so small. It seems like there's a coin inside."

"Could be..." Mrs Shaw said again.

It didn't take long to pull the wrapper away. Helen held up a shiny disk. "What is it?" she asked.

"Look more closely and you'll see."

Helen scrutinised it carefully. "It's got writing on it... Mum! It's got 'Sam' written at the top followed by our address and phone number!"

"Of course. It's his identity disk in case he ever gets lost."

"That's fantastic!" Helen said, and gave her mother another huge hug. Then she crouched down beside Sam. "Come on, friend. We've got to get you organised." On went the collar, with the disk attached by a small ring. Even the lead was tried out, Sam patiently walking round the room beside Helen's heel. "Well done," Helen congratulated her puppy. "We'll let you try out the food bowl a little later."

The lead was taken off, but the collar and disk left proudly in place round Sam's neck. "Now everyone will know he's mine," said Helen.

"I hope you didn't mind your birthday gifts being for Sam," said Mrs Shaw.

"Not at all," Helen answered. "They're the best gifts I could have had."

Suddenly she paused. A thought had formed in her mind, and as she grasped it, she wondered how she hadn't realised something ten minutes earlier when the first present was opened. "Mum," she said. "These presents - they were all here this morning. You must have got them last week. How could you know that I was going to buy Sam? I might not have been able to."

Mrs Shaw smiled. "Your Dad and I talked and prayed long and hard about that, Helen. All I can say is that you're not the only one in this house who has faith. We began to know that you were meant to have Sam, so we bought you these presents."

"Phew…" Helen said. "That was a big risk, Mum. Weren't you scared?"

"I did have my moments, especially this morning!"

"You must have done…"

"But having faith about something always involves some risk. You don't need faith if something is guaranteed."

"Thank you for having faith about Sam," Helen

said. "And I'm so glad to have parents like you."

"We're glad to have a daughter like you." Mrs Shaw felt her eyes go moist. "Enough of all this," she said, smiling tearfully. "It makes me want to cry. There's one more present here for you - Wendy handed it in the other day."

This one was flatter, and Helen didn't have too many problems guessing it was a book. And she had the paper off in no time since Wendy only put one layer of wrapping on her presents. With astonishment in her voice Helen read out the title. "'Caring for your first puppy'. What a fantastic present for Wendy to give me. How could she be sure?"

"Maybe this business of having faith is infectious," Mrs Shaw laughed.

Helen laughed with her. "Not a bad disease to catch."

"There's one more gift from your Dad and me," her Mum went on, "but I'll need a moment to fetch it. Why don't you wait for me in the kitchen, and while you're doing that you could have a little look in the cupboard above the sink."

Helen couldn't make any sense of that instruction, but so many other puzzling things had turned out well that she wasn't going to argue. "Come on, little chap," she said, picking Sam up and heading for the kitchen. She knew the cupboard her mother meant. It was the one where they kept all their cans of soup or baked beans. Helen had no idea why she should look at them.

She opened the cupboard door. There was the soup, the beans, and plenty of other tins. Her eye moved along the shelf until it rested on some tins she had never seen before. "Puppy food!" she shouted. "Look Sam! That's for you! You're not going to be a hungry puppy after all." Now Helen knew why her mother had been so reluctant to do any shopping after they left the hospital. Everything was already in stock.

"It's all fantastic Mum," she shouted as she heard her mother returning. "Thanks!"

"I'm glad you like it, and I hope Sam does too," Mrs Shaw replied, speaking loudly from the other room. "Now, close your eyes - and Sam's too - and I'll tell you when to open them again."

Helen buried Sam's face into her arms, and shut her own eyes tight. There were a few muffled sounds, as if her mother was struggling to move something. This had to rank as the most dramatic and mysterious birthday she had ever had.

After what seemed an age, her mother said, "Okay, you can open your eyes now."

Helen blinked - and then blinked again! On the floor in front of her lay the most beautiful dog box she'd ever seen. Each side had a couple of panels of finely sanded wood. Bright red cloth covered the floor of the box. Helen bent down, and it was wonderfully soft. It had been padded with foam, and the padding ran half way up the sides to give its occupant a bed which would be warm and comfortable all round.

No words came from Helen. Mrs Shaw answered the question Helen couldn't manage to ask. "Your Dad made it during this last week. That's what he was busy doing in the shed over several evenings. It looks good, doesn't it?"

"Good? It's incredible!" Helen laid Sam down into his own box. "There you are Sam. You're going to have the most luxurious bed of any dog anywhere."

"He's a fortunate little fellow," Mrs Shaw said. Sam seemed to agree. He turned himself round two or three times, and then curled into a tight ball and went off to sleep.

Helen stood up beside her mother. "I don't know how to thank you and Dad. This has been the most extraordinary and wonderful day of my life. This last week has been like nothing else I've ever known."

"I think that's true for me too," sighed Mrs Shaw. "I'm so happy for you Helen, but I don't know that I'd like to go through it all again...!"

"No, neither would I." Helen looked down at her puppy. "Sam's here now, and he's content. We don't need to."